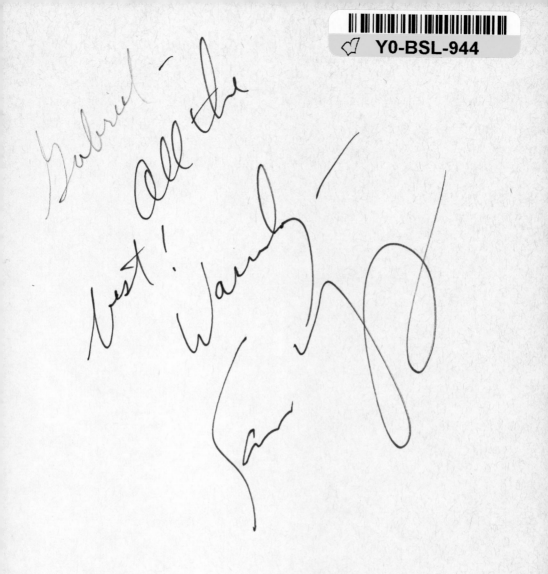

Gabriel —
All the
Best!
Warmly

Strategies for Success
in Real Estate

Strategies for Success in Real Estate

SAM YOUNG

Reston Publishing Company, Inc.
A Prentice-Hall Company
Reston, Virginia

Library of Congress Cataloging in Publication Data

Young, Sam.
  Strategies for success in real estate.

  1. Real estate business. 2. House selling.
3. House buying. 4. Real estate listings. I. Title.
HD1375.Y665 1983   333.33'068'8   82-21634
ISBN 0-8359-7080-9

10 9 8 7 6 5 4 3 2

Printed in the United States of America

Illustrations by Bruce Bolinger

To Seaborn and to Ann
for showing me the way
and making me believe that I could.

Contents

Preface

How can an author say all that he wishes about his work and still remain within the limits of modesty and good taste? I shall endeavor to do so but make no promises.

This book represents more than a successful approach to selling residential real estate. It is a logical, highly effective series of programs and techniques that, when applied, will produce most impressive results. The question becomes, How can they produce enormous earnings for the reader? That is the byproduct of the information in this book combined with the reader's creativity and personality. The true secret to ultimate success in real estate sales is to apply effective and proven methods of producing listings and sales (this book) with the special qualities that make one unique. It sounds so simple that most fail to see the depth. Can there possibly be a more winning combination than an effective game plan and a genuinely sincere effort? Assuming the reader is prepared to make a genuinely sincere effort, let's examine why this book is an effective game plan.

This book brings to the real estate agent an inventory of alternatives, alternatives that will produce tremendous amounts of business for individuals who apply them. They are representative of the practices of the most successful and productive real estate salespeople. Approaches are presented in a step-by-step fashion so that the reader can follow a guide for a technique's implementation. This book's purpose is to have the technique understood by the reader as well as acted upon. Not everyone will be willing to put into practice all that I have shared; that is understandable. All that is necessary is to be aware of the alternatives so that each individual is truly able to make the best choices for himself or herself. I have not attempted to say what one *should* do but rather what one *could* do. The choice, as always, is up to the reader. One takes from this book what one wishes; if applied consistently, it will be effective. The more one takes, the more productive one will become.

Every section of this book is relevant and/or adaptable to any geographical area. It only requires the creativity and personality of the individual. There is no attempt to suggest the memorization of any of the dialogues given to illustrate the use of techniques. I do not believe in "canned" sales approaches. We have spent our entire lives becoming who and what we are. We must build on our strengths rather than attempt to remake ourselves into someone we are not. One should take the personality that he or she has developed and expand upon it. Researchers in education have found that memorization is a very sterile and temporary form of learning. Therefore, I suggest a planned approach to allow the individual to follow the proper steps to reach a desired outcome, in his or her own words.

This book makes no attempt to discount the intelligence of either the public or the agent. People are smart and, if made privy to accurate and complete facts, will reach proper and prudent decisions. Within this book I expose varying approaches to the many activities of agents; at no time do I ask anyone to do anything not based on logic and fact. There is no dogma within this book; no idea is expressed without reasons for its effectiveness. Nothing in this book must be done out of blind faith. Unless the effort being suggested makes sense to the agent, he or she will not apply the technique consistently.

Additionally, every program in this book is presented in a logical fashion from the public's point of view. There are no tricks or ploys to cause the customer or client to do anything that is not, in his or her judgment, prudent. Manipulation in selling is completely absent from this work.

This book is designed to help everyone regardless of the level of experience or production. Following the direction given throughout this book will prove a most productive addition to one's career. It is purely a matter of making the choice to apply the material. This book will help increase income, effectiveness, and efficiency.

Sam Young, GRI/CRS

Acknowledgments

It is with grateful appreciation that I acknowledge the following individuals and organizations. Through their work, publications, printed material, books, films, and courses they had an indelible effect upon my life and career. Their influence is apparent within areas of this book. It is with everlasting gratitude that I mention:

Houston Board of REALTORS®
National Association of REALTORS®
REALTORS® National Marketing Institute
Texas Association of REALTORS®
W. Steven Brown
Dr. Fitzhugh Dodson
J. Douglas Edwards
Julius Fast
Alan Lakein

I would further like to express my gratitude to Robert P. Robinowitz, whose invaluable help contributed to the development of the illustrations in this book, and to Susan G. Speer, whose conscientious efforts in typing this manuscript allowed me to meet all deadlines.

sellers after they agree to list and the buyers after they agree to buy. Of course, we must stay in touch with the sellers, constantly advising them of their position in the marketplace, what has transpired with the property since the last conversation, the presentation of offers, etc. We must arrange an appointment with the mortgage company or savings and loan, introduce the buyers to the loan officer, follow up on the processing of the loan to avoid needless delays, take the buyers to the house numerous times after they sign the offer but prior to their taking title to the property so that they can measure for furniture. We are assuming that overall we will spend an equivalent amount of time with the sellers after they agree to sell as we do with the buyers after they agree to buy. Therefore our time concern is really the time to get the listing versus the time to make the sale. From researching many real estate salespeople from all parts of the country, I have found the following averages.

1. In obtaining a listing, the average experienced agent spends three hours with a seller in order to get the listing agreement signed. If we divide the $1,200 ultimately earned from this saleable listing, we see that the agent is actually earning $400 per hour for every hour spent with a willing seller who lists.

2. No one who actively solicits listings obtains all of them. We will only obtain a percentage. The average rate of success in the group that I researched was 33⅓ percent. In other words, they would go on three listing appointments, attempt to list three different willing sellers, but obtain only one listing. If we apply this success factor to the previously determined hourly rate of $400, we find that they are earning $133.33 ($400 ÷ 3) per hour for every hour spent face-to-face with sellers, whether securing the listing or not.

To appreciate the magnitude of this rate of per-hour earnings, it must be measured against the selling effort's per-hour remuneration. Further research has shown the following.

1. It is not uncommon to spend an average of 12 hours with buyers before they agree to buy. Compare this with the amount of dollars earned ($1,200 ÷ 12 hours) in our earlier example; it results in a per-hour-earning rate of $100 when we make the sale.

2. Just as with listings, we don't sell every buyer. On the average we are finding that salespeople are selling approximately one of every five buyers. If we apply this to the per-hour rate of $100, we find that every hour spent selling is worth $20 ($100 ÷ 5), whether we make the sale or not.

This is the bottom line. What is time worth every hour spent listing as opposed to every hour spent selling? In the preceding examples, time is almost seven times more valuable listing ($133.33 per hour listing versus $20 per hour selling). While obviously these averages and ratios will not be true of each salesperson, it will serve as a structure to follow in determining the true value of an agent's time. Although average price transactions, commission schedules, and cooperating commission splits vary, it is rarely ever more profitable per hour to sell rather than to list.

PRIORITIES AND PRIME SALES ABILITY

We should never forsake listing in favor of selling. When we do, we only delay the degree of success that we could be enjoying. Of course, the best things are the most difficult to get. It takes far more sales ability to list than to sell. Listing requires the greatest amount of creativity, conviction, and ability to communicate.

How much sales ability is needed to sell a house? No magical or mystical words can cause people to buy a home that they don't want. Regardless of an agent's persuasiveness and control over buyers, no one invests tens of thousands of dollars in a home that he or she doesn't like. The real strength in selling is in placing the purchasers in the home that best suits their needs, wants, desires, and finances. If a person were looking for a home and drove by a residence having an open house, walked in and fell in love with the house because it was exactly what that person wanted (area, type, style, floor plan, schools, price, etc.), rest assured a sale would be made. It wouldn't make any difference who the agent was, whether or not one had ever heard of the company, how old or new the company was, or how many agents were associated with it. All that mattered would be finally locating the right home. On the other hand, if a person were going to sell a home and an agent came out to talk about listing, answers would be needed to questions: "Why should I list rather than sell it myself?" "Why should I deal with you as opposed to some other company?" The true art of selling is necessary to handle this situation effectively.

While some people are better at showing houses than others, we must recognize that in no way are we using as much sales ability when we sell as when we list. Justifiably, we will never earn as much when we sell as when we list. Only if the agent is willing to accept this challenge and arm himself or herself with proven step-by-step techniques for improving effectiveness in both areas, will he or she achieve tremendous success.

2

Where Listings Come From

Having recognized the enormous potential for earnings from listing, one must consider where to acquire them. There must be many alternatives available to the individual in pursuit of listings. One of the biggest problems that the agent encounters is overworking one source of listings and then one day the well runs dry. The agent must then cultivate new sources. By the time the new sources have begun to show results, much time and money have been lost. The secret to success in any area of sales is to maximize one's alternatives.

SOURCES OF LISTINGS

One of the great aspects of pursuing listings is their countless sources. This book apprises the reader of specific techniques to use in pursuing various sources; this chapter is specifically designed to identify a number of the sources.

It is impossible to list all the sources of listings. Every idea can develop a source. There is no bad source of listings. Obviously some sources will prove more fruitful than others, but no source is unproductive for the creative salesperson.

The next section discusses the concept of "brainstorming." We shall see its application to the expansion of one's sources of listings. For now let's take a look at some of the sources:

- **For Sale by Owners** (FSBO). This is the most obvious

source of listings available. The seller is expressing a need or desire to sell by virtue of the FSBO status.

- **Current Buyers**. The buyers with whom one is working represent a significant number of sellers. Most buyers in the marketplace are already property owners and will usually have a property to sell in order to buy another property.

- **Past Buyers**. The buyers who have bought from the agent and the agent's company are most likely, based on the national average of homes selling every five years, to be sellers within four to six years of their purchase.

- **Local Papers**. There is a wealth of business in a local newspaper. Every announcement that an individual is being transferred or has been promoted or has had a birth in the family generally will be followed by investment in a new home. This, of course, means the old home will have to be sold.

- **Seller's Neighbors**. Whenever a home goes up for sale in an area, it is always interesting how many others go on the market in the next 30 days. The neighbors of the current listings are a great source.

- **Savings and Loans**. While savings and loans do not necessarily pass along listings on foreclosures to agents who bring them loans, since all agents are doing that, they are more likely to do so when the agent makes a special effort to build rapport with the loan officer.

- **Attorneys**. Probate attorneys or those handling estates are in a position to direct much business to an agent.

- **Architects**. When people have an architect design a new home, the architect becomes a good source of referrals for the old homes.

- **Accountants**. As with an attorney, the accountant knows the tax position of his or her clients. When the advice to sell property is given, it would be nice if, in addition, the agent's card were given to the client.

- **Moving Companies**. Who is in a better position to know when someone needs to sell a home than the people who handle the move?

- **Doctors and Dentists**. When people move to another city, they generally inquire of their doctor and dentist for the name of another in the new city. It wouldn't be difficult for him or her to give the patient an agent's name to handle the sale of their home.

- **Corporate Personnel Departments**. Major companies that transfer executives all over the country always want to make the move as easy as possible. Many companies have special departments that handle everything for the transferred employee, including the selection of the agent to sell the house.

- **Insurance Salespeople**. When people decide to move, one of the people contacted is the insurance agent who handles the homeowner's coverage on the home. This is a good source of listings.

- **Builders**. Since many people who buy homes have property to sell, builders are dealing daily with people who are potential listors. This can be one of the best sources.

- **REALTOR®s in Other Cities**. While the idea of making contact with REALTOR®s in other cities is nothing new, the active pursuit of these potential sources is generally neglected. When buyers inspect another community where they are considering moving, the REALTOR® with whom they will be working is in a great position to make a recommendation regarding the marketing of their existing home.

- **REALTOR®s in Other Parts of the Community**. It is generally accepted that a REALTOR® is unable to service properly a seller who lives outside that REALTOR®'s market area. Yet often for-sale signs on houses indicate REALTOR®s well outside their geographic area. It is, of course, each individual REALTOR®'s opinion as to what is within a geographic area, but there is certainly nothing wrong with approaching REALTOR®s in other areas of the city and setting up a referral agreement. In doing so, one is able to refer between one another to everyone's advantage. There will also be cases in which a smart move would be to contact the REALTOR® whose sign is on a house in an area well outside of the listing REALTOR®'s market area. During this conversation, one might advise the listing REALTOR® that should marketing the subject property be a burden, he or she would be happy to accept the listing and pay the agent the normal referral fee. While this may not be enthusiastically embraced by some REALTOR®s, it is a wise consideration and a good move for all.

- **Banks**. Of course, numerous departments in banks know when someone is moving. The most obvious is the individual who handles the transfer of funds. Frequently when individuals move, they will go to the bank with whom they have their accounts and request that the bank give them a letter of credit or a similar form indicating that they have funds on deposit and are creditworthy, which they can take to the bank in the city where they are moving. The new bank will generally request the balances in the customer's accounts be transferred. The people who handle this aspect of customer relations are a valuable source of listings.

- **Mail Carriers**. Often mail carriers are asked questions by people who are considering moving, as to the proper procedure in having mail changed to another address. A good contact with a mail carrier can be one of the greatest contacts.

- **Hotels and Motels**. Practically everyone goes to a hotel or motel for a place to stay when going to a city to look for a home. The people who work behind the front desk are a tremendous source of business, since they are usually asked for the name of a REALTOR®.

- **Friends and Relatives**. As discussed later, the amount of business available through the people whom friends and relatives know is staggering. The proper approach in this area can be amazingly profitable.

BRAINSTORMING FOR LISTINGS

The tremendous number of listing sources available are locked away in each reader's mind. Regardless of whether one has any real estate experience, an agent can produce a vast number of listing sources with only a little effort. The effort is to apply the principle of brainstorming.

In brainstorming one simply takes a tablet of paper and at the top of each page writes a letter of the alphabet. Starting with *A*, the job is to write down everything that comes to mind beginning with that letter. Some of what is written will not directly relate to getting listings, and that's okay. The idea is to reduce to writing as much as one can, and then consider whether those mentioned have any relationship, directly or indirectly, to real estate sources. If they do, they should be pursued. If they don't, they should be eliminated. In the end, there is a long list of possible sources for listings.

For example, start with the letter *A*:

A

Apple	Alter Ego	Attorneys
Architects	Ambivert	Accountants
Animals	Arrest	Art

Examining the preceding list, we can eliminate the following:

~~Apple~~	~~Alter Ego~~	Attorneys
Architects	~~Ambivert~~	Accountants
Animals	~~Arrest~~	~~Art~~

We are left with the following sources for listings:

Architects	Alter Ego	Accountants
Animals	(Psychologists)	
(Veterinarians)	Attorneys	

Through a simple method of allowing the mind to flow freely, recording all its thoughts, and then eliminating those that do not apply and changing those that trigger another thought, one is able to produce a tremendous number of results.

Exercise

Using the brainstorming method, produce an additional 20 sources of listings other than those mentioned.

3

Door-to-Door
Public Relations

Despite all the sources of listings available to the real estate agent, none has the potential of door-to-door public relations. Referred to in many circles as *farming*, this technique of producing record numbers of listings has proven time and time again a major contributor to the success of top producers. By *top producers*, I am not referring to those people who consistently earn a living in real estate sales but rather those who are among the top 5 percent of salespeople, the superstars. They are superstars because they do things in their careers that cause others to sit in awe. These people are often thought of as *workaholics*, driven because of passions that are without comprehension and financially successful at the sacrifice of themselves and their families. In reality, they differ little from anyone else in the real estate industry. Most have no greater ability than those who earn far less. Many often enjoy a richer personal and family life as a result of being able to afford to do more with their free time. The difference is that because of their clear understanding of the nature of the business and their willingness to capitalize upon the vast opportunities available to them, they simply leave the others far behind.

DOMINATE AND CREATE CONTINUITY
WITHIN AN AREA

The primary objective of such door-to-door work is to capitalize upon the existing business in an area. Through consistency, one can create a continuity within a neighborhood and ultimately become the dominant REALTOR®. Whenever people decide to sell their homes, they want to deal with someone who has credibility and knowledge of their area. The greatest way to become the person whom they seek out is by literally going out and meeting potential clients. Personal acquaintances are an important influence when seeking advice. Getting to know the homeowners before they need a REALTOR® is the secret to the success of this program. This is important to realize because our real goal is not to go into an area one day and see how many listings we can gather, but rather to go into an area and make a favorable impression upon the homeowners in the area so that they will think of us when they have the need of a REALTOR®.

Will they need a REALTOR®? Nationally, homes are selling every five years. The days of living in a home all one's life are a thing of the past. Peoples' tastes and circumstances change; before long a home no longer holds all the comfort and benefits that it once did. Job opportunities and advancement for employees necessitate relocation. This takes place to such a degree in many areas of the country that homes are selling at a much more rapid rate than the national average. Some areas are experiencing a turnover rate of as much as 33 percent (houses selling on the average of every three years). People will eventually need a REALTOR®. It is this knowledge that makes the entire program justifiable.

There is another interesting facet to be considered: the REALTOR® trend. In any given week one should compare the number of new listings submitted to the local multiple-listing service with those available as for-sale-by-owners. There are an infinitely greater number of homes going on the market with REALTOR®s than FSBOs. This trend is gratifying to the industry as a whole, but is the reader getting his or her share of these listings?

With fewer and fewer homes available as FSBO, how can one get a share of those listings going directly to REALTOR®s? Some agents feel that having friends in the area is the answer. Having friends who live in an area is certainly a benefit because they can, if they will, give input as to neighbors who may be moving. However, most people don't hear of their neighbors' plans to move until after the decision has been made and the house has already been placed on the market. As mentioned, getting to know the homeowners before they need a REALTOR® is the secret. Door-to-door PR work is not only the vehicle, but is essential to the continued success of real estate agents and companies alike.

VALUE OF AN AREA

The only way for a salesperson to achieve that desperately sought plateau of security in the real estate business is through door-to-door PR work. Only when one has a hold on a healthy share of the market can one maintain a secure feeling about one's income. Otherwise, it is a daily battle.

If we take a closer look at the potential earnings within an area, we shall be better able to appreciate the true value of this aspect of listing real estate. For example, let's use an area of 400 homes. If we apply the annual rate of turnover in the home market of 20 percent (homes selling on the average of every five years), this area or subdivision of 400 homes would have 80 sales every year. Giving the for-sale-by-owners the benefit of the doubt, let's say that 10 percent (8) of the transactions are done by FSBO. This means that 72 sold listings are handled by REALTOR®s. If we apply the average commission earned from each transaction of $1,200, established in Chapter 1, we find that these 72 sold listings generate $86,400 in annual listing commissions ($1,200 × 72). That's $86,400 in listing commissions paid directly to real estate agents in one year in a 400-home area.

While we can't expect to get all the transactions in an area, we can expect to get a substantial share. If we could get approximately 20 to 30 percent of the business in such an area, it would mean an extra $17,000 to $25,000 a year. When it grows into 40 and 50 percent, we can truly appreciate the meaning of the expression, "how sweet it is!"

TIME COMMITMENT NEEDED

Surprisingly, this program can be accomplished in less time than one might think. The key is to be committed to the program and allocate a reasonable amount of time to an area consistently without interference. One must select an area compatible with the amount of time allocated to it. For instance, before scheduling 2 hours a day, 20 days a month, to an area of 400 homes, one should determine whether it will work. Assuming that one can, in fact, make the 20-day monthly commitment (the other days taken up with conflicting appointments, days off, closings, etc.), this will mean 20 homes per day. With two hours to cover 20 homes (120 minutes ÷ 20 homes), one can spend 6 minutes at each house, more than enough time to make the whole program work effectively. The main factor is to find the amount of time that one *will* spend in an area and then adjust the size of the area to fit the time allotment. Should one find that this time allotment is, for some reason, not sufficient, a decision must be made. Either one finds more time for the area or reduces the area to fit the time. One must always be realistic and avoid establishing a goal out of proportion with the time available. Otherwise the area will not be adequately worked, produce little or no results, and be abandoned because the program won't work. This program will work in every area if it is coupled with determination, creativity, and persistence.

STEPS TO REAP THE REWARDS

1. Select an Area

In area selection, two considerations should be given: (a) Is there a good annual turnover rate among the houses (only research of past years' activities can disclose this); (b) Does any one REALTOR® have a large share of the listings? If the area chosen is one with a low turnover rate, obviously other areas should be considered. Likewise, if one REALTOR® seems to have the lion's share of the listings in the area for the past year (50 percent +) then perhaps another, undominated area might show more immediate results. No area is so tied up that it can't be penetrated. However, an area with a large number of REALTOR®s actively competing for listings, with no one in control, would be better and show more immediate results.

2. Inventory the Area

An agent should drive through the area and check for-sale signs. One should list all houses available by owners or REALTOR®s. (If one deals in leasing, those for rent should be included.) Then the agent should check the multiple-listing service (MLS) for those available through REALTOR®s perhaps without a sign. Last, one should check the classified section of the newspaper for any other houses that might be available but weren't represented in the areas checked thus far. A complete list of all properties available for sale by either the owners or REALTOR®s should be developed. This list should then be transferred to index cards, with one house per card.

3. Color Code Each Card

Each card should be color coded for immediate identification. Adhesive stickers can be purchased to place at the top of each card and, with the following code, will differentiate them: red—FSBO; blue—for sale by other REALTOR®; and black—for sale by the agent's firm. (Those handling rentals should utilize three additional colors for rentals available by owner, REALTOR®, the agent's firm.) At this point, one has a complete inventory of everything available within the area of specialization.

4. Preview Available Properties (FSBO)

The FSBOs must be contacted immediately and appointments set up to inspect each property. The specifics on listing a FSBO are covered in a later chapter.

Figure 3-1.   Sample FSBO Inventory Card

5. Preview Available Properties (REALTOR®s)

Contact should be made with each listing agent on the available homes in the area in order to arrange a preview of the property. (In doing this, the rules for obtaining such appointments should always be followed. For those unsure of these rules, the local multiple-listing service should be contacted for clarification.) Upon previewing each home the basics about the property and the features within that home unique for the area should be noted on an index card. A sample is given in Figure 3-1. This card is also used when previewing FSBOs. Should it be listed by an agent's own company or another company before it sells, the appropriate names can be filled in at the time. The color coding avoids confusion (Figure 3-2).

Blue Code

Property Address 1010 Elm

Owner's Name John & Mary Smith

Owner's Phone # 555-1212

Listed By ABC Realty

Agent's Name Jane Doe

Phone # 555-1515 Home # 555-2121

Date Previewed 10/4 How Long On Market 5 days

Comments: 4 BR 3 Baths 2 car Gar/C.P. Trad. Style

Fireplace Woodburning Type Construction B/V Roof W/S

Terms: Cash or Assumption Price: $98,000

MLS Info: Wooded lot, wet-bar in m/B, pool, loan balance — $60,000 @ 9%. Total payments $650.00

Figure 3-2. Sample Inventory Card

6. Update Records

In order to keep the inventory (step 2) current, the area should be reviewed every day. (One should check for new for-sale signs, new ads, new listings in MLS). If there are new listings by REALTOR®s, they must be inspected immediately. If there are new FSBOs, the agent working the area should be the first agent to call the owners. If one is truly specializing in the area, he or she must be closer to the area than anyone else.

7. Include Future Listings

Each of the homes not on the market should be recorded on an index card. Utilizing the cross-reference directory (a directory that lists, by addresses, the names and telephone numbers of the individuals residing at those addresses, providing they have published telephone numbers), the name and telephone number of the homeowners should be noted on each card. This can be done on the day preceding the visit to the area for those homeowners to be called on. Therefore, after a complete round of the area, the reference cards will be complete. All contacts and information on each home should be recorded on each respective card.

```
Property Address  210 Walnut
Owners  Hal & Jennie Perkins
Phone #  543-2112
Style Colonial  Exterior  B/V  Roof  Comp.
Children's Names  Larry - 6yrs. old
Contacts And Comments  10/1 - Leaving for
School Outing  11/3 - Not home
12/1 - Asked about price
neighbor received for Their home
```

Figure 3-3.   Sample Future Listing Card

As these houses begin to go on the market, the previously mentioned index cards (step 5) should be filled in, and the card attached to it.

8. Use a Tickler File

Since subsequent visits and their frequency are critical to the success of the entire program, some form of reminder should be utilized in order to assure consistent followthrough. A tickler file is an ideal method for achieving this goal. Once all homes have been recorded on index cards, a small file box should store these cards. If one's plan is to be in the area 20 days a month, 20 dividers should be placed in the box, separating the number of houses (20 in this example) to be contacted each day in the area. As a day's visit to the area is completed, the used cards should be placed in the back of the box, leaving the next group of houses in front, to be used during the next visit. After that day, the procedure is continued, so that the cards for the next group of houses are at the front and those for the group just visited are at the back.

9. Contact Acquaintances and Send Letters of Introduction to Homeowners

Before making contact in the area, the agent should determine (via the cross-reference directory) those whom he or she may know in the area, regardless of how well acquainted. There is a great opportunity to cultivate these individuals for referrals and, of course, make them feel somewhat special by being advised of the agent's activity in the area before anyone else knows. This is immediately followed by a letter of introduction to each homeowner in the area (Figure 3-4), which should be received before any contact with the first 20 homes. The purpose of this letter is to let all the homeowners know immediately of the agent's activity in the area. It should tell who he or she is and what he or she does, and to expect a visit. While direct mail produces poor results, it is the only method available to let the homeowners who may not be visited until the end of the month know of the agent's efforts and availability. Should any of these individuals need a qualified agent prior to the visit, at least there is a chance, remote as it is, that he or she may call. If no such mailing is made, there is no chance at all.

Date

Mr. and Mrs. John Doe
1010 Elm
Anywhere, U.S.A. 11111

Dear Mr. & Mrs. Doe,

My name is _____ with _____ Realty
Co., and I am proud to inform you that I am specializing in your
neighborhood.

If I can ever be of assistance to you, your family or friends with any
real estate needs, please don't hesitate in contacting me.

I look forward to meeting you personally in the coming month.

Sincerely,

Figure 3-4.   Sample Letter of Introduction

10. Visit Each Home Monthly

The primary ingredient in this program's success is consistency.
The goal is to go through the area completely, visiting each home
once a month. Since the objective is to make personal contact with
as many homeowners as possible, the time of day for the visits is
important. This is something that only trial and error will reveal
The makeup of every area is different, and the habits of the inhabi-
tants of each area are equally inconsistent. However, one can discover a pattern to the activities of the residents and within a relatively short period of time be able to zero in on the best time of day
to find the greatest number of people at home. As a starting point, I
would recommend about one hour before the schools dismiss
classes for the day. Most people who don't work (and even those
who work part-time) will try to be at home when their children are
due from school. Again, this is not true in every part of the country,
but it is a good, logical place to begin.

Sample dialogue for initial visits follows.

First Visit

AGENT: *Hello, is Mr. (or Ms.) Jones at home? (Present giveaway to the homeowner; see step 11.) Mr./Ms. Jones, my name is John Doe with ABC REALTOR®s. How are you today?*

HOMEOWNER: *(Response)*

AGENT: *As I mentioned in my letter to you, I specialize in residential real estate in your neighborhood. If I can ever be of assistance to you, your family, or friends, please don't hesitate to contact me. (Pause in case they wish to respond.) Have a nice day.*

Second Visit

AGENT: *Hello, Mr. (or Mrs.) Jones. (Present giveaway.) I'm John Doe with ABC REALTOR®s. I met you last month. How have you been?*

HOMEOWNER: *(Response)*

AGENT: *We've just put the Smith's home on the market at 1010 Elm and I wondered if you have any friends or relatives you'd like to have for neighbors?*

In the event that the agent's company has not listed anything in the area, the agent should use one of the competitor's listings but not indicate that it is his or her company's listing.

AGENT: *The Nelson's home at 22 Bellaire has just been placed on the market. I wondered if you had any friends or relatives you'd like to have for neighbors?*

HOMEOWNER: *(Response)*

AGENT: *It's nice to see you again. Have a nice day.*

Third Visit

AGENT: *Hello, Mr. (or Mrs.) Jones. (Pause, and make a reintroduction if necessary.) I'm John Doe with ABC REALTOR®s. (Hand the homeowner a giveaway.) How are you today?*

HOMEOWNER: *(Response)*

AGENT: *We've just sold the Smith's home at 1010 Elm. There were so many people interested in this neighborhood, I wondered if you knew of any of your neighbors who might be interested in selling their property?*

In the event that the agent's company has not made a sale in the area, the agent should use one of the competitor's sales but never take credit for a sale if credit is not due.

AGENT: *The Nelson's home at 22 Bellaire has just been sold. There were so many people interested in this area, I wondered if perhaps you knew of any of your neighbors who might be interested in selling their home?*

HOMEOWNER: *(Response)*

AGENT: *Thank you and have a good day.*

This is only a structure. One should put this message in one's own words. The individual makes it work. After the third visit, there should be ample topics for conversation, such as new schools to be built in the area, new shopping centers, etc. The important consideration is to keep the visits short.

One should *never ask for the listing*. Though the homeowners somewhat suspect that the true purpose of the visit is to obtain the listing ultimately, which is true, the agent must avoid posing this question. If the question is asked, and response is *no*, there is no reason to return to that home. Their suspicions are confirmed; future visits will be met with considerably less receptiveness. One must keep in mind that no homeowner needs a REALTOR® until selling the house; neither the agent nor the homeowner knows when this will occur. One thing is certain: it will occur.

11. Leave a Gift at Each Home

The more one can do to make a lasting impression on potential customers and clients, the better. In order to help achieve this and to help create an atmosphere conducive to one of the agent's primary objectives (meet and get to know the people), a giveaway should be given to all homeowners visited. This psychologically obligates them to receive the agent as long as it is a brief encounter.

When the giveaway is presented to the homeowners, it should be done while greeting them, and no mention should be made of it. Further, it should be hidden in some form of cover so that its identity cannot be readily determined. If the agent expresses that he or she has something for the homeowners or hands it to them so that they can identify the gift, they will usually express a flat refusal. Every salesperson involved in any kind of direct sales uses a giveaway. The agent should strive to be different in the approach to the customer. Instead of referring to the giveaway, either verbally (commenting on it) or nonverbally (exposing it), the agent should simply hand the envelope (containing the giveaway and a business card) as he or she begins to speak. The most amazing thing then takes place. The homeowner takes it. We always take what is handed to us, particularly if it is enclosed in something.

In view of the large number of giveaways to be used, it shouldn't be too expensive but must have some usefulness to the homeowner. Many companies have a wide variety of such giveaways available for their associates, but the agent should develop his or her own. Doing what everyone else does has never proven to do more than duplicate the success of everyone else. If one looks at the average income of the average agent in the community, I doubt that it would be an acceptable amount. Being different, standing out from the rest, is a great asset, if done in a positive and professional way. There are numerous giveaways from which to choose. Contacting an advertising specialty company can help. Some giveaways that have proven useful are key chains, scratch pads, pencils, rulers and yardsticks, potholders, calendars, book covers, emergency-number stickers for the telephone, and note magnets for the refrigerator door. All giveaways should identify the company and the agent. How this is done would be best accomplished through discussions with the broker and an advertising specialty company. The identity of both the company and the agent should be represented as subtly as possible.

One problem with every giveaway is its potential life. How many key chains can a person use? How many potholders can a kitchen stand? What is the maximum number of calendars that a home can endure? It is necessary to rotate giveaways to avoid repetition. I would certainly be remiss if I did not share my best giveaway: recipe of the month. This type of giveaway is useful, different, and inexpensive. One can use recipes for hors d'oeuvres, salads, entrees, desserts, gourmet meals, drinks, or anything else that would be well received in the area. Every month features a different recipe, and many people look forward to them. But they must be good recipes. One could get the recipes from someone who has a reputation for good cooking.

12. Follow Up Each Visit

After making the day's contacts, notes should be sent to all the homes visited whether someone was at home or not. Those people at home are thanked for the time spent with the agent; those not at home receive the message by mail that the agent would have expressed verbally.

This follow-up to visits is like the icing on the cake. How many times does one go shopping and receive a thank-you note for *not* buying? It makes a fabulous impression on homeowners. They meet the agent today and get a thank-you tomorrow. Personalizing this note makes it even more meaningful. Sample follow-up notes are given in Figures 3-5 and 3-6.

Date

Ms. Jean Jones
1234 Beech St.
Anywhere, USA 11111

Dear Ms. Jones,

Just a note to thank you for taking the time to talk with me when I stopped by on Monday.

I look forward to serving you.

Sincerely,

P.S. I hope that your garage sale was a success.

Figure 3-5. Sample Follow-Up Note — Contact at Home

Date

Mr. & Mrs. John Jones
4321 Young St.
Somewhere, USA 12121

Dear Mr. and Mrs. Jones,

I am sorry that you were not at home on Monday when I stopped by
to introduce myself, but hope you make use of the recipe that I left
on your door.

As I mentioned in a previous letter, I specialize in residential real
estate in your area. If I can be of assistance to you, your family, or
friends, I hope that you won't hesitate in contacting me.

I look forward to meeting you next month.

Sincerely,

**Figure 3-6. Sample Follow-Up Note — Contact Not at
Home**

13. Visit Those Who Were Not at Home on Weekends

Though the note to the ones not at home will be helpful, it will not
replace the impact of personal contact. A month will pass before we
are to attempt to find them at home again. Therefore, if at all possible, one should visit these individuals over the weekend. This must
be put into the overall plan to order to maximize the impact and
thereby maximize the results. The cards for this group, each properly noted with the activity that has transpired on each, are then filed
in the tickler file for next month.

CREATING A HIGH PROFILE IN AN AREA

The repetition of contacts in an area will serve more than anything
else in gaining credibility, name recognition, and, of course, more
listings. Additionally though, one must constantly be thinking of

new and different ideas to make lasting impressions on the home-owners.

Many people are of the opinion that every effort should be made to educate residents in an area as to the talents and the competence of the company. I differ with this line of thinking, slightly. While I am the first to agree with the need on the part of REALTOR®s to do all that we can to make customers more aware of the value of our services and the ends that we go in an effort to procure a sale, this is not necessarily the lone message with which to inundate the public. Because most people do not think the same as current buyers and sellers, they don't place as much importance on the areas that most REALTOR®s spend endless amounts of time and money communicating—the services that they provide. Obviously, if one needs a REALTOR®, he or she is more cognizant of those benefits. However, to one not currently needing those services, "REALTOR® propaganda" goes in one ear and out the other. The agent must remember that he or she is not engaged in an advertising program but rather a rapport-building program. Therefore, one must have more to talk about than business. If not, the agent will soon become like those individuals constantly trying to sell something to their friends. Every time these individuals are with a friend, they talk only about their product or service. They never call just to talk, no visit is ever made without the ulterior motive of bringing up business. Their friends begin to avoid them.

This is analogous to the agent who does nothing in his or her area except talk business. It is necessary to combine the Door-to-Door PR work with other activities in the area in an effort to become part of the community. Due to the monthly visits, the agent is in a position to learn much about the residents in the area and can take advantage of various occasions (birthdays, anniversaries, etc.) to make more and more personalized contacts which enhance his or her image in the neighborhood.

Numerous programs can be initiated; I have listed some suggestions. Agents should develop some of their own that are more geographically oriented and tied to upcoming activities in the community.

January—Happy New Year Balloons

For a modest sum, an agent can do something that will absolutely be the topic of conversation in the area for weeks. Brightly colored balloons are printed with the following message:

HAPPY NEW YEAR
JOHN DOE
XYZ REALTY CO.
YOUR REALTOR

One balloon is placed in front of each home in the area, between the hours of 3 a.m. and 6 a.m. on New Year's Day. Each balloon is filled with helium, put on a six-foot string, and secured to the ground at the curb of the residents' homes directly in line with the front door. The impact on the residents is unimaginable. One can just picture himself or herself getting out of bed on New Year's Day after a fun-filled New Year's Eve, going to the front door to get the morning paper, and seeing big, brightly-colored balloons up and down the block, wishing everyone a Happy New Year.

February — Valentine Drawing Contest

One of the greatest vehicles for getting one's activities known in an area is the neighborhood children. Therefore, much of what an agent does should be directed at children. One way to begin is a contest for the nicest valentine. Notice of this should be mailed in early January, with awards based on originality, execution, and content. The winners should be announced on Valentine's Day and prizes awarded. It is best to have a disinterested third party do the judging; the judge and the contest rules should be announced at the outset. The judging occurs at the agent's office, where pictures can be taken of the winners and their parents and submitted to the local newspapers. It's amazing how much attention the media will give to a human interest event such as this.

March — Saint Patrick's Day Party

Arrangements should be made with a conveniently located school to hold a party on Saint Patrick's Day there. Schools will generally allow this, and often at no charge, as long as the party area is cleaned up afterward. A couple of parents should serve as chaperons; attendance should be restricted to those wearing green, with a special award for the best outfit. The agent can serve punch and cookies, hire a local actor to dress like a clown, and let the kids enjoy themselves for a couple of hours. This produces lots of pictures and lots of attention by the media, as well as the parents.

April — Easter Egg Hunt

Easter eggs should be placed all over the neighborhood. The residents should know that the eggs will be there on Easter Sunday for their children to find. If the area is visited that day, one will find dozens of children hunting for the Easter eggs. Again, media coverage is a natural. The agent must remember to call the local newspapers beforehand.

May — Mother's Day or Memorial Day Cards

This has a particularly nice effect and keeps one's presence known.

June — Flag Day Notices and Father's Day Cards

Notifying the residents that Flag Day is approaching and encouraging them to fly the American Flag is not only a patriotic gesture but also an excuse to make contact. Father's day cards to the fathers in the area provide continuity.

July — Fourth of July Notices

Wishing everyone in the area a Happy Fourth is another opportunity for contact. Well-designed flyers or cards are adequate.

August — Back to School Giveaways

A well-received activity is the distribution of book covers, pencils, etc., to school children. These are useful giveaway items and allow additional contact. The ads on these items go a long way.

September — Labor Day Cards

A simple card wishing everyone a pleasant Labor Day weekend is effective.

October—Halloween Activities

There is no limit to what one can do around Halloween. Pumpkin giveaways are always popular. This can be followed by a pumpkin carving contest to determine the best jack-o-lantern, with judging on Halloween Night while the jack-o-lanterns are lit in front of the homes. Not only does this allow the judge to see the jack-o-lanterns at night, but also it makes a definite impression on the neighborhood.

November—Election Day, Veterans Day, and Thanksgiving

Any number of activities can be centered around these events. Notices can remind people to vote for the candidates of their choice and list where and when to vote. Voters' registration drives in the area are always good for the neighborhood and draw attention. Veterans Day cards can be sent to those whose family members served in the armed forces. Thankgiving cards should be sent to everyone in the area.

December—Christmas Cards/Giveaways

Seasons greetings cards should be sent to the residents in the area. Another extremely effective promotion during December is to invite all the area parents to bring their children to some centralized location (a school or shopping center parking lot) to receive a gift from Santa Claus. For a very modest expense, one can hire a Santa Claus for two or three hours to ask the children what they want for Christmas and give each of the children a candy cane. If the neighborhood residents are properly and adequately notified, this can be an extremely successful event.

Area Newsletter

As time goes by and as more and more information about the people living in the area (i.e., birthdays, anniversaries of the purchase of a home, graduations, weddings, etc.) is collected, one will be in an excellent position to develop an area newsletter, with timely information of interest to the people who reside in the area. The key for a successful newsletter is to remember that it must contain information worth reading. If not, it only becomes junk mail. To get an idea for the format to use, an agent can consult a local public relations company to find the type most effective for the area. Many times this can be accomplished through a telephone call.

With a little thought, the agent can develop many more ideas for the area. The important thing is to decide what can be used. One should not overload with programs that become too expensive and require more organization than feasible. One should start with a workable schedule and couple it with consistent monthly contacts, gradually adding to it until reaching the saturation point in the area. By *saturation point*, I mean enough programs allowing the agent to reach everyone in some form or fashion. The yardstick for measuring these programs will be the degree of success in acquiring listings. An accurate record must be kept of all listings on the market, with whom, and the agent's percentage. By watching the share of the market (the percentage of the current listings that are the agent's), one can track one's penetration. The greatest strides come after the first year.

As mentioned, there are tremendous rewards for the agent who can persevere. Over the next five years, there will be transactions equivalent to 100 percent of the homes in the area. Hundreds of thousands of dollars in commissions will be paid to REALTOR®s; probably no agents will have a conscientious program to secure this business. The agent who decides to go after this business will have little competition. It isn't easy and doesn't happen overnight. But, if the agent can incorporate it into his or her work life and maintain consistency, success is inevitable.

Exercise

Using the information contained in this chapter, plan the initiation of door-to-door public relations work. Be specific with regard to area, timetable, frequency of contacts, type of giveaways, etc. No part of the program should be implemented until the complete plan has been formulated.

4

Creating Referral Business

The most desirable position for the real estate agent is working with a great deal of referrals. I have used the words *great deal of* as opposed to *exclusively with*. I do so in an attempt to reinforce the need to avoid dependency upon any one area to produce income. Should one deal exclusively with referrals, one has ceased to develop new business and is only taking care of the existing business. This can and does often cause complacency and is the first sign of an oncoming sales slump.

Anytime we give up control of what happens in our lives and place it in the hands of others (i.e., former customers, friends, relatives, management, etc.), we are destined for a letdown. When this letdown occurs and one becomes aware of the need to take other action to avoid a drop in productivity, time is lost. With this lost time comes lost production. One who can manage the greatest number of alternative sources of productivity will produce the greatest amount of earnings.

WHAT ARE REFERRALS?

Referrals are generally considered any form of business resulting from anything other than direct contact with the customer, such as customers and clients who are referred by others (friends, relatives, former customers, business acquaintances, agents in other cities, etc.). Frequently included are those former customers who call on the agent to assist them again as a result of being pleased with an experience of either selling or buying through the agent. This latter group of former customers is actually repeat business. I make this distinction because repeat business comes after a few years in real estate sales. If one is relatively new, repeat business is not a readily productive source; however, referral business is. We shall address the creation of referral business and save the cultivation of repeat business for another chapter.

Referral business is that business resulting from the recommendation of another. Another commonly used expression for the creation of a referral business is *cultivating centers of influence.* Centers of influence are those people in a position to know when someone wants to buy or sell property (architects, accountants, attorneys, friends, relatives, etc.). What one chooses to call it is moot, as long as the program is implemented.

DOLLARS THAT SLIP AWAY

Before we begin to examine the procedures to create a profitable referral business, we should pause to examine the true potential of such a program. In almost every market, the average person annually meets 2 people who want to buy or sell a home. If the average agent is acquainted with 100 people (regardless of how well), these 100 individuals will have contact with individuals involved in 200 transactions (100 × 2 = 200). If we apply the average commission established in our example in Chapter 1 ($1,200), this means that these 200 transations represent $240,000 in commissions to agents ($1,200 × 200 = $240,000).

What share of this business lands in the pocket of any one agent? On the average, I would venture to say less than 2 pecent. Most agents do not possess the program nor the inclination to acquire a healthy share of this business.

PEOPLE-TO-PEOPLE PUBLIC RELATIONS

Due to the necessity of establishing the proper rapport with people in order to put oneself in the best position to be recommended to those needing a REALTOR®'s services, I call this effort people-to-people public relations (P-T-P PR). Public relations is a major part of the agent's efforts. One must basically do the following.

- Determine whom he or she knows.
- Divide this list into workable groups.
- Establish goals with each group.
- Follow the steps that make the program work.

Whom Do You Know?

This is a simple question but not quite simple to answer. It is difficult because most people are unaware of whom they really know. We can make a list of all the people involved in our everyday lives, but what about those who are part of our lives but not on a day-to-day basis? The reader should make such a list and have other members of his or her family make a list as well. This list should include *everyone* known, regardless of how well. After this list has been compiled, it should be compared with the list made by the other members of the agent's family (spouse, parents, children, etc.). All duplications should be eliminated. All lists should be used to make one master list.

Divide and Conquer

This list should be divided into workable groups. This is necessary due to the different relationships with different people on the list and different objectives with each.

There are basically four groups with which to work:

- Closest friends and relatives
- Other friends and relatives
- Acquaintances
- Adversaries

Closest friends and relatives are those individuals who care the most about one and one's future. These people will go out of their way to help because they genuinely care about the agent. Unfortunately, this is one of the smallest groups. It does not take long to determine those in this group. Generally, these are the people who, if given the opportunity, will voluntarily recommend the agent to someone in need of the services that an agent renders. They don't need to be asked.

Other friends and relatives are those individuals, for whatever reason, not chosen for the first group. These are most relatives and friends on a social basis. These people are more than acquaintances but perhaps not near and dear. They would not so eagerly and voluntarily give one's name to someone who needed such services unless a direct request were made of them.

Acquaintances make up the largest list. One meets so many people in this category. These people are aware of who the agent is but are not so well acquainted with the agent that they would recommend him or her even if asked. This is not due to any harbored animosity but rather the distant nature of the relationship and the superseding of another REALTOR® with whom they are more familiar.

Adversaries are those individuals (usually among former customers) who, for no valid reason, feel hostility toward an agent as a result of some event, possibly during a transaction, for which the agent was perhaps innocent but for which they hold the agent responsible. While one would like to believe that such individuals do not exist, one cannot be in any business very long without someone being unhappy with one for unjustifiable reasons.

Goals for Each Group

With the list divided into four groups, the next step is to establish goals for each group. We later discuss exactly what to do with each group, but now we want to establish goals.

Group 1 — Closest Friends and Relatives

One needs to get them to work actively on the agent's behalf. As mentioned, this is the smallest group of people, but each agent knows whom to call comfortably about asking for help in finding business. Most people wouldn't think twice about calling parents or a close friend and saying, "Hi! I've got a problem and I need some help. I've got a new listing that I really need to sell. Could you see if any of your friends know of someone looking for a new home?" These are one's closest friends and closest relatives; there should be no problem in making such a request. If people are listed in group 1 whom the agent would not want to ask this, they must be put into another group.

Group 2 — Other Friends and Relatives

The agent should draw on them and attempt to move them in to group 1 (in terms of what one can expect from them). This group is made up of people who, if asked, would recommend the agent. The agent should strive to motivate them to volunteer a recommendation without being asked.

Group 3 — Acquaintances

One should draw on them and attempt to move them into group 2 (in terms of what one can expect of them). We had established this group as those who would not recommend the agent even if asked. Therefore, the agent wants to change this so that, when asked, this group will recommend him or her.

Group 4 — Adversaries

These should be neutralized. The fear is that an agent's customer might converse with an adversary and possibly hear some unflattering statement that could damage trust and confidence in the agent. This is a real danger when dealing with customers who work for a company that also employs someone in group 4. By neutralizing these individuals, one can drain the reservoirs of hostility and hopefully circumvent any such problems.

STEPS TO MAKE THE PROGRAM WORK

The overall objective of this program is, in addition to securing referrals for the agent, to create an image of one who is an authoritative voice on real estate. This is only achieved by action supporting this claim. This is best achieved by the implemetation of the following.

Mailings

An agent should create a mailing to be used at least twice a year. Usually the only mailing an agent makes to all potential sources of referrals is at Christmas. While mailing Christmas cards is fine, I am referring to a different type of mailing. We are trying to establish ourselves as the authoritative voice on real estate; this is never achieved by a holiday card. An ideal way of accomplishing this is through the use of a real estate newsletter. Two things are important when structuring such a mailing: It must be of interest to the reader and it must be worth reading.

Therefore, the information regarding the agent's company and its services must be limited. While the home buyer and seller should know all the fine attributes of the firm, this is of little interest to someone not needing such services. The people receiving this newsletter are those from whom the agent wants referrals, not those whose personal business is wanted. While a great many of them will eventually buy and sell through the agent, the purpose of these contacts is to cultivate referrals.

To achieve this, mailings must be directed to what will interest the readers. Articles on the previous quarters' effect on property values are always of interest to property owners. Changes in the community that will directly affect future property values will always prove timely. Articles must be applicable to the area. Newspapers and magazines provide articles that would be good for the newsletter (*Note*: When taking something from a newspaper or magazine it is advisable to quote the source such as "according to the *Wall Street Journal*," "*Time Magazine* reports," etc.).

The wonderful part of this program is that, with the exception of originating the mailing list, none of this must be done by the agent. For a nominal expense one can retain a local company specializing in the preparation of newsletters and have it not only prepare the newsletters but also address, stamp, and mail them. Many direct-mail companies also prepare newsletters. These companies also have mailing lists for sale. A quick call to the Better Business Bureau or Chamber of Commerce will locate them. If no such company is available locally, perhaps a journalism student at the local college might prepare such a mailing. The agent must only review the content to ensure its compatability with the agent's own ideas. Of course, national companies do newsletters. The consideration when selecting such a company is the relevance of their information to the specific area. These national firms are certainly worth considering, particularly if no other alternative is available.

While the amount of dollars expended for such a mailing must be budgetable, it is foolish to shortchange oneself on the quality of the newsletter. We have already established that there is a potential of $240,000 in earnings among the recipients of the mailing; the impression made on them will be greatly impaired by a substandard format and inexpensive paper stock. The same is true for the way the newsletter is printed.

Personal Contacts

Personal contacts should be made a minimum of twice a year. In addition to the use of a real estate newsletter, one must plan on making a personal contact (either in person or by phone) at least twice a year for the specific purpose of asking for business. Agents are often in a quandary as to the "right" way to get business from their friends and relatives in a social situation. There is no proper and acceptable way to do this unless they bring up the subject. Some people take this to mean that one must be around all the time, attending all events, so that when the question of real estate comes up, he or she is there to give the answer. Should one take this course of action, it places the agent in a most unattractive position. He or she is again the dependent individual, only handling what comes his or her way (not to mention the enormous amount of time that all this socializing requires).

Therefore, there must be certain, designated calls for the purpose of asking for business. Though it may sound strange to have planned calls for business, one must consider the alternatives. If one intermittently asks for business, one of two things usually occurs. Either the agent asks so seldom that he or she gets no results, or the agent asks so frequently that no one wants to talk to him or her.

However, by scheduling a minimum of two calls a year to each person on one's list, the agent never becomes overbearing. The calls should be staggered between newsletters. Ideally, the agent mails a newsletter in January and phones in April. In July, he or she mails another newsletter and phones again in October. As a result, one has some kind of contact every three months. While the agent must personally make the calls, this will not be a time-consuming project. If one has 100 people on this list, by simply making 3 to 4 calls a day the agent will complete the calls in one month without any need to alter the normal work schedule. If, however, one waits until the last few days to make all 100 calls, the agent will be on the phone constantly each day.

The conversations should be simple and brief. After the pleasantries, the dialogue should be something like this.

> *Mary, it has been so nice talking with you, but before we hang up, may I ask if you have any friends or relatives who might be interested in buying or selling property?*

It takes no more than that. Depending upon the response, the agent will either take the name of the referral or thank the person and encourage keeping him or her in mind.

Thanks anyway and please keep me in mind should you hear of anyone.

I can't make it more difficult than this; it's just that simple. If there are a few people on the list that an agent just can't ask this of, then they should be removed from the list. If an agent doesn't want to ask this of anyone, then I recommend determining what is blocking that person (insight might be found in *The You That Could Be* by Dr. Fitzhugh Dodson). There is no reason for anyone to avoid asking another for business. Merely determine in what fashion one would be the most comfortable in doing so and surge ahead.

For group 4, we can best accomplish this objective by combining a sincere attempt to resolve the sensitive area of the relationship with the individual along with all the mailings and phone calls that we are planning to the balance of the list. In our conversations with this group we must bypass any effort to gain a referral and concentrate on healing old wounds. Many times this can be best accomplished when the agent faces the individual over coffee or lunch. Such action can easily defuse pent-up hostilities.

Supplemental Mailings

In addition to a newsletter and phone calls, I highly recommend other mailings. The agent may wish to mail certain bits of information about himself or herself and the company (newspaper clippings of awards, outstanding sales volume, etc.). These should be brought to the attention of everyone, but separately from the newsletter.

Holiday cards are effective in keeping one's name before people and should be sent throughout the year. While Christmas cards are fine and should be sent, these cards tend to lose their impact because of competition with all the other Christmas cards received. I believe in sending cards on other occasions as well (New Year's, Valentine's Day, Easter, Fourth of July, Labor Day, Thanksgiving, etc.)

ONE VERY IMPORTANT POINT

After receiving a referral, in addition to thanking the individual for the referral, one always advises them on the result. Nothing is worse than making the effort to do a favor and then never hearing from that individual again.

The end result of these ideas, combined with one's own creativity, is to experience a level of productivity once thought reserved for those with much experience. The agent who doesn't implement this type of program will in time experience some referrals, but never in the magnitude enjoyed as a result of this technique.

Exercise

Plan a detailed one-year people-to-people PR program, utilizing as many of the ideas mentioned in this chapter as possible. Include additional ideas of your own in an effort to make the most effective overall program. The program should be planned so that someone unaware of this approach could implement this program from the plan.

5

The For Sale by Owner

If one were to gather a cross section of experienced sales associates and ask them how they felt about listing the for sale by owner (FSBO), one would probably hear responses such as:

> Oh, they're okay for the new associate who doesn't have much business, but I'm so busy I haven't got the time to call on them.

> Why go to a FSBO? That's where everybody looks for listings. The secret is to go where the others don't go.

> FSBO's are a pain. If they wanted to list, they wouldn't be FSBOs to begin with, so why beat your head against a wall?

None of these responses has much validity. Those who feel that they are too busy to call on FSBOs always seem to have enough time to work with a new buyer. The agents who feel everybody goes to the FSBO are only perpetuating a misconception in this business. Actually, very few people attempt to list FSBOs. Many agents "call" a FSBO but few actually go to the home of the FSBO and make a listing presentation. The opinion expressed by those who feel that FSBOs are a waste of time voices hidden feelings of inadequacy, covered up by the attitude that "if people wanted to list they wouldn't be FSBOs."

If one continued with this cross section of REALTOR®s and asked them to be honest in their response to the question, "How many of you have made listing presentations in a FSBO's home more than once in the last 30 days?" the response would amaze.

About 2 percent will respond affirmatively. This percent statistic comes from my research during travels conducting seminars across the country and noting each group's response to that question. Rarely have I seen more than 2 percent affirmative from any group (ranging in size from 10 to 1,000). What is the reason for this overwhelming resistance to soliciting the FSBO? The answer is *attitude*, pure and simple. Our attitude toward whatever we do has a direct bearing on how well and how often we do it.

This statistic nullifies the idea that everyone goes after the FSBO. Why do so many FSBOs comment on the tremendous number of agents who have called? The key is in the last part of the question, "tremendous number of agents who have called." Granted, lots of agents call but only about 2 percent have enough drive and belief in themselves and their mission to see the FSBO face to face.

If by some freak occurrence the agents call, optimistically they must then be able to withstand the infecting impact of the attitude expressed by the FSBO—statements such as "Thanks, but we want to sell it ourselves"; "We're not interested"; "When we're ready we'll call you." Even when the agent hears something to the effect of "You can come out and look at the house and we'll pay you a commission if you sell it but we want it clear that we are not going to list," he or she will approach the FSBO with great reluctance, based on the belief that this seller is not going to list and the agent is wasting time.

It must be understood that the FSBO is a FSBO because the owners don't know why they shouldn't be. They have determined, based on whatever line of reasoning (commission, being tied to one REALTOR®, etc.) that their interests will be best served by avoiding the REALTOR®. The FSBO is not considering everything.

The professional REALTOR® certainly knows why people should not try to sell their own homes. Why can't he or she recognize that the public has the same capacity for understanding as the REALTOR®? If only they were made privy to the same input that shaped the attitude of the REALTOR®, there would be no more FSBOs.

It is far too generous an attitude to assume that the REALTOR® knows why a FSBO should be listed with a REALTOR®. One can only conclude that the average REALTOR® does not in fact know just how prudent it is to have one's home listed exclusively and that the seller can usually net as much if not more in spite of the fee. Perhaps it would be best to examine these advantages in detail.

It is a fact that the more people one has to sell something to, the higher the price, and the fewer people one has to sell something to, the lesser the price. It is an accepted fact that if the market for a particular product or service narrows, the price must also drop. This is exactly what occurs in the case of the FSBO. There are only four basic ways that a FSBO can hope to market a home in an effort to reach the public:

1. An ad in the paper
2. A sign in the yard
3. An open house
4. Contact with friends in hopes of a referral

This reaches a dramatically small number of buyers, when compared to what the REALTOR® can do, it is almost insignificant.

The services of each real estate company, of course, vary. If we take only one aspect that most REALTOR®s do have — multiple listings — we see immediately a vehicle for exposure beyond equal. I have never believed that MLS in and of itself is ever enough reason to list with a REALTOR®. But, since it is offered by so many firms, let's look at its impact.

If the average agent has at least 2 buyers with whom he or she is working at all times and if there are 200 members of MLS, that totals 400 potential buyers who could be made aware of a property if it were in multiple listing. Of 400 buyers, the odds are very great that one will want the sellers' home. It also, by virtue of the 400 buyers, immediately widens the seller's market. Aren't the odds greater that of 400 buyers, the seller will have his or her property shown to someone who wants that specific home as opposed to what comes from the FSBO attempts? Won't someone who wants everything in a particular home pay more for it than someone who wants only the general aspects (i.e., the buyer who wants three bedrooms, parquet floors, close to a hospital, on a bus line, must have a finished and heated garage due to need of having an office in it, and extra wide halls as a result of a dependent in a wheelchair, versus the buyer who doesn't care much beyond three bedrooms)?

Consequently, the REALTOR®'s ability to locate the right buyer for the right home is what gives the REALTOR® the advantage in finding the buyer who will pay the most for the property and consequently allow the REALTOR® to net the seller as much, if not more than, the seller could net himself or herself without any of the problems and inconveniences.

So strong is my belief in the advantage of dealing with a REALTOR®, that I carry it a step further. If homeowners have an appraisal made on the home, what they receive is actually a distorted picture of its worth. When appraisers are called upon, they will compare the subject property to other comparable properties that have recently sold. These comparables are generally obtained from REALTOR®s and they are all REALTOR® transactions. To my knowledge, there is no record of FSBO transactions. Therefore, the sale price that the FSBO can expect for his or her property will be less than the appraised value *unless* he or she utilizes the same kind of marketing plan used in the sale of the comparable properties. It is actually an incorrect assumption on the homeowner's part to anticipate getting the same price as another homeowner who utilized a REALTOR®. The marketing efforts of the REALTOR® were responsible for the price paid for the comparable properties, not the existence of the property.

It should be noted that our fine appraisers are not to blame. The REALTOR® is. The agent is remiss for not bringing this to the attention of the homeowner. If sellers want the absolute most money for their property when they want to sell, they should seek the services of a reputable REALTOR®.

In this section, we are going to discuss the approach and technique for obtaining an appointment with the FSBO and everything up to the listing presentation itself, which is covered in the next chapter. The reason for this division is based on the belief that there are two specific parts in obtaining a listing from a FSBO. One is getting the appointment and the other is making the presentation.

WHY THE FOR SALE BY OWNER EXISTS

Before we can intelligently examine the most effective approach to the FSBO, we must look into the reasons for their existence. The most obvious reason is, of course, an effort to save the commission. While this is the biggest motivator for the FSBO's continued existence, there are others that should be considered. Basically, there are four main reasons that FSBOs exist:

1. **Desire to Save Money.** Every homeowner is interested in, as he or she should be, netting as much as possible from the sale of the property. At first glance, it would appear that bypassing the REALTOR®'s fee is an obvious step in that direction.

2. **Lack of Basic Trust.** Many people have, unfortunately, a distrustful attitude toward salespeople. We must be aware of this problem and be prepared to deal with it.

3. **Seller Pride.** There are some people who have had much experience in the world of selling. Due to unfamiliarity with what is necessary to sell homes, they approach the sale of their home with the attitude that they are just as capable of selling the property as anyone and want to try their hand at it.

4. **Bad Past Experience.** As long as there are people, incompetence will exist. As long as it exists, the competent people must be prepared to defend themselves from the problems caused by the incompetents. In this situation, the seller takes a course of action due to unsatisfactory results or experiences in the past.

One must be sensitive to these four aspects so that the initial contact with the seller does not immediately go against what the seller believes to be the best approach for him or her in selling the home. If it does, the only opportunity to see the FSBO will be wasted.

GETTING READY

Every day the agent should check the newspaper for properties offered by owners. (For the best utilization of time, this should be delegated to a secretary or done by the agent at a time that doesn't conflict with other activities.) Each should be noted on a FSBO sheet; names, addresses and phone numbers should be included, along with information from the ads. Most communities have cross-reference directories available listing houses by address and by phone number (except for unpublished phone numbers). If all this information is not in the ads, it should be obtained before any contact.

The agent should always be on the lookout for FSBO signs in travels around the city in an effort to stay on top of the FSBO market. These properties should be added to the FSBO list if not already included.

GETTING THE APPOINTMENT WITH THE FSBO

There are basically three effective approaches to obtaining an appointment with the FSBO: (1) arranging an introduction; (2) calling for an appointment, and (3) dropping by unannounced.

Arrange an Introduction

This is an effective but rarely used method of obtaining an appointment. In doing a little research, we can determine, by use of certain cross-reference directories, the places of employment of individuals who live at the address of the FSBO property. In many cases, we are able to find sellers who work for companies also employing our acquaintances. In this case, a simple phone call to the acquaintance, requesting help in setting up an appointment with the homeowner can result in the best kind of appointment: the third-party referral. This is not applicable in every case, but a little effort will prove rewarding in more instances than one might think.

Call for an Appointment

If the preceding step proves fruitless, the agent should consider calling for an appointment. This often results in the most desirable circumstance since, when successful, we are able to set up a time convenient for all parties involved. In the case of properties involving more than one owner, this will put the agent in contact with all parties necessary to make a decision and save a tremendous amount of time.

This aspect of getting an appointment with the FSBO is not called *call for an appointment to list* but rather *call for an appointment.* Our objectives are clearly *not* to make the call for the purpose of listing the house as much as to view the property. In good conscience we cannot honestly say that we are calling a FSBO to list it, when we have no idea what the property is like, how much the seller desires to receive for the property, what the marketability of the property is, etc. These decisions can be made only after the agent has seen and inspected the property. However, some agents and readers of this book may take issue with this position.

We must first ask ourselves, are we willing to take any listing on any property at any price? Most probably we are not. If one can agree, for instance, that one would not list a $70,000 property for $100,000, then consider this. If one calls a FSBO and asks for an appointment because the agent wants to list the seller's house, he or she is actually making a false statement. The statement indicating that the agent wants to list the house should actually state that the agent wants to list the house providing the house meets certain criteria (i.e., price, accessibility, cooperative attitude on the part of the seller, availability of financing, etc.). To make such a statement to the FSBO seller who doesn't feel he or she needs a REALTOR® only drives the seller from any consideration of allowing the agent to view the property.

Therefore, we must reevaluate the *real* reason that we are calling and all the benefits to be derived by all parties (seller and agent) and present this to the seller as a valid reason for an appointment. Recognizing the FSBO's desire to avoid a REALTOR®, what are the benefits to all involved of having the agent view the property if no listing is obtained? From the agent's viewpoint there are many.

1. **One becomes aware of the competition.** FSBOs are definitely competition to listed properties. It would be nice to know that should one of the agent's buyers end up in the hands of a FSBO, the FSBO represents no threat.

2. **Build rapport.** We can begin to establish rapport with the seller. This can ultimately lead to business, be it listing the seller's property, selling the seller a new home, or getting the names of the people to whom the seller has shown the house and selling them another home.

3. **Creating a sale.** If we have exhausted everything listed but are still unable to locate a home for a buyer, and we feel sure that the buyer would be interested in the FSBO's house, are we going to allow the buyer to find the FSBO? To avoid this, the agent should again attempt to list the FSBO. If unsuccessful, and with no other alternative, the smart agent will get a listing protecting the agent for a one-time showing so that the agent can attempt a sale. (This should not be done unless all other means of locating a home for the buyer and listing the seller's home have failed.) It is the only alternative. This is particularly true when we discover, in point 1, that the competition is a real threat.

From the sellers' viewpoint, if they can continue to show the house themselves and still have the advantage of a possible sale by a REALTOR® at a figure that will net the sellers what they want, they have the best of both worlds.

Since all these benefits are real to both seller and agent, the best approach on the phone is to work from this position, the one to which the seller is going to be most receptive and the only one that the agent can, in good conscience, take prior to viewing the property and determining all the facts. I offer the following technique.

AGENT: *Hello, Mr. (or Ms.) _____?*

FSBO: *Yes.*

AGENT: *Mr. (or Ms.) _____ , this is _____ with _____ REALTOR®s. I understand that you have your property on the market, and I thought perhaps I could be of assistance.*

FSBO: *Well thank you, but we're not interested in using a REALTOR®.*

AGENT: *I understand and I'm sure you have had a barrage of REALTOR®s calling, haven't you?*

FSBO: *As a matter of fact, they've been calling all day.*

AGENT: *Well Mr. (or Ms.) _____ , I'm not calling about listing your house.*

FSBO: *Then why are you calling?*

AGENT: *The reason that I am calling is that from time to time we find ourselves in a position when working with a buyer, particularly an out-of-town buyer, where the homes that we have on the market and those available through the multiple-listing service are just not sufficient to satisfy the needs of the family. When in this position we'd like to be able to show an owner's home, and if we can show it at a figure that will net the sellers what they want and still pay our fee, why we can benefit each other, can't we?*

FSBO: *I guess so.*

AGENT: *Could I come by this evening at 7:00 or would 8:00 be better?*

FSBO: *I believe that 7:00 will be best.*

We must analyze what we have done in using this technique. We have made only true statements and have shown the sellers that we can provide them with a service compatible with their position as a FSBO. We have said, "I am not calling about listing your house," which we established as completely true. The idea of listing can only be based on a complete understanding of all the facts related to, and a complete preview of, the seller's property. Therefore, we are truly not calling about listing the house.

We have told them, "From time to time we find ourselves in a position (in other words this does not happen very often) when working with a buyer, particularly an out-of-town buyer (we work with out-of-town buyers, which is to whom every seller wants to sell his or her house) when the homes that we have on the market and those available through the multiple-listing service are just not adequate to satisfy the needs of a particular family, and when in this position we'd like to be able to show an owner's home (we show our houses first, then we show what's available in MLS, and then, and only then, do we show an FSBO). If we can show it at a figure that will net you what you want and still pay our fee, why we could benefit each other, couldn't we?" (If I can bring you a contract on your property at a figure that nets you what you want and you didn't have to list, you have only benefited yourself.)

All this is completely true. This is the most acceptable approach to a FSBO in hopes of an appointment. The most important thing is not to allow speculative pessimism to cause an agent to discount this approach. If one thinks, "What happens when you get to the house and it's overpriced as it is, and you can't get that price, let alone one that includes your commission?" or "How are you going to bring up the subject of listing after you've said you're not calling about listing?" — these are valid points. They are dealt with later in this chapter. The most important point is that we have made a phone call to a FSBO and have made truthful statements reflecting the mutual benefits of an appointment. If the reader has problems with this approach, I must suggest rereading the subheading "Call for an appointment." It clearly provides all reasoning behind the validity of this technique and must be understood completely and with deep conviction, or this technique will never be applied properly and its potential success never truly realized.

At this point, no rational seller can say *no* to this technique. It is too logical and provides the seller with the best situation possible, from the seller's frame of reference. However, occasionally there is a response of "No thank you, we want to sell it ourselves." Such a response is illogical and would appear as though the seller were not listening. At this point we must try to understand what is going on in the mind of the seller, as almost all people with whom we deal are bright and this response isn't reasonable. Probably, a situation exists where husband and wife have decided to sell their house themselves and have agreed to tell any REALTOR® the pat answer "No thank you, we want to sell it ourselves." Without consideration of what was said, this unreasonable response comes out.

At this point, the only remaining alternative dictates that the agent must psychologically put the seller in the position of turning down this benefit. It is easy to say *no* to something that has not yet happened. We must ask the following with great sincerity and much tact.

> *I understand how you feel, but just to clarify my thinking, if I had a buyer for your home, and though I have many buyers I have not seen your home and have no idea if I have one for your house, but if I did, and they would pay enough for your home to net you exactly what you want, you would prefer that I sell them someone else's house, is that right!*

The response to this question may very well be, "I'll have to speak to my wife." This says that he is interested but because of this prior agreement with his wife, he must talk to her before he can agree to allow the agent to come to the house. At this point one should try to get an appointment to explain it further to both. If this is rejected, one should try to get the wife's phone number and call personally. If this also fails, the only alternative is to allow the husband to speak with her and call back. Regardless of the final outcome, the agent has made greater inroads to obtaining the appointment and has greater understanding of statements of sellers that often are labeled irrational and cause the agent to drop the FSBO as not worth dealing with.

Drop by Unannounced

This technique is felt by many to be the best approach to the FSBO. It gets right to the individual who has the decision-making power and does so on a face-to-face basis. However, there are potential problems. When one goes directly to the door of the FSBO unannounced, the agent has no way of knowing whether both husband and wife are at home, or whether he or she is going to the home at the most opportune time. This course of action eliminates the alternative of calling for an appointment if the seller tells the agent that he or she is not interested and "don't call us, we'll call you."

If, however, one is unsuccessful in obtaining an appointment with the seller on the phone, one can always utilize this alternative and drop by the sellers' house and leave information about the services of the agent's company, information that the owners should consider when selling a home, etc.

The most important aspect of obtaining the appointment with the FSBO is that it be truthful, beneficial to the seller, and low-keyed. Incorporating all three of these aspects into the approach to a FSBO will bring a high percentage of appointments.

INSPECTING THE PROPERTY
AND BUILDING RAPPORT

These two areas go hand in hand. The initial stages of the relationship with the seller are the best times to build rapport. The impressions made during this formative period are generally unchangeable. As a result, one should be careful to avoid any kind of interaction that could raise barriers. Since the inspection of the property should occur during the first part of the meeting between the seller and the agent when in the seller's home, this is the ideal time to combine the two.

Upon arrival at the sellers' home for the appointment, the agent should carry as little as possible. The sellers are anticipating the agent's arrival and are somewhat prepared in terms of attitude, which is at best one of apprehension. Generally unacquainted with the agent, the sellers are somewhat guarded toward him or her. Regardless of how the sellers project themselves, they know that the agent is in the business of selling real estate and have their sales resistance operating unconsciously. When encountering this kind of situation, the less one can do to run true-to-form in the preconceived image of salespeople, the better. One step in that direction is to eliminate those aspects of one's appearance indicative of salespeople.

Thus, the agent should begin by carrying only what is absolutely necessary for the appointment (i.e., legal pad, pen, listing agreement, estimated closing statement, MLS forms, office forms that must be executed at the time of listing, etc.). This should be placed in a compact case, not the enormous briefcases that so many agents carry (they look like small suitcases).

One must try to eliminate everything indicative of the typical salesperson. One is not there to perpetuate the image of a salesperson but rather to project an image of a professional real estate counselor. In doing this, one must create the best atmosphere, one that is relaxed and totally unthreatening.

Consistent with this desire to be less threatening, one should carry this beyond appearance. One should avoid coming on like a salesperson. This can occur frequently, and one must attempt to become aware of such occurrences in an effort to make the conscious decisions to change how one ordinarily interacts with customers.

What does the average agent usually do when the seller comes to the door? As the door opens, the agent usually introduces himself or herself, extends a hand, and offers a card. Let's examine the impact of this brief and damaging interaction. First of all, it is typical of just about every type of salesperson; second, it accomplishes far less than the damage it causes. While we have all been raised to extend our hand to someone we don't know, this is best left undone when in a selling situation. Such a gesture, when initiated by the salesperson, only confirms the preconceived belief of the customer about the person coming to see the house—a "salesperson" is coming. Couple this handshake with offering one's card and the agent has successfully eliminated most hope of overcoming the initial barriers between salesperson and customer. As we present ourselves, so we shall be received. If one comes across as a salesperson, one can expect to be thought of as a salesperson.

What harm could possibly occur if the agent were to go to the door, knock, and, when the seller answers, smile and introduce himself or herself without initiating the handshake? The answer is absolutely none. This would also be the case if one avoided offering a business card at the time. The obvious reaction on the part of the seller to such a low-keyed approach is one of ease and gentle relief. Most of the time, at this point the seller will extend a hand, to which one will respond. The difference between the effect of the agent's response to the seller's handshake versus the seller's response to the agent's is the fact that the seller initiated it. Should he or she request a card, the agent obliges.

Upon first meeting, one must treat all people as though they are introverts, until they prove themselves differently. In Julius Fast's book *Body Language*, he makes it quite clear that "touching" in its most innocent form can, with some people, create barriers that are sometimes impossible to overcome. The same is true of any action consistent with that of an individual whom one would just as soon avoid. The kind of salesperson to whom most people are accustomed is not one with whom most people are interested in dealing. As a result of years of conditioning, the sudden elimination of gestures, mannerisms and expressions is difficult, but not impossible.

After the introductions, the first goal is to preview the property with the seller. Since previewing is an excellent opportunity to build rapport, one should make every effort to have the seller show the agent the house. This is usually no problem, but when sellers suggest that the agent look at it alone while they are watching television in the family room, the agent must initiate something to encourage them to go along. This is usually best accomplished when the agent gives the seller a reason beneficial to the seller.

Mr. Seller, since I'll be taking lots of notes about your house, I'd appreciate very much your showing me the house so that I don't miss anything you're particularly fond of.

When inspecting a house, the agent must see everything to be considered in the purchase of the property. If one is timid about opening the sellers' closets or built-ins, one might preface the tour of the property with the following.

Mr. Seller, in an effort to avoid missing anything, I'd like to look at your house through the eyes of the most discriminating buyer. Would that be alright?

This will not meet with disapproval, and one can more comfortably inspect the seller's house.

There are five main parts of the inspection of a house:

1. **Record the tour.** There is no greater way to remember all the important features of a home than by writing them down. While inspecting a property, the agent should make notes about everything. This will not only trigger one's memory but allow one to recall the affect of a particular feature. As an option to writing everything down, one might use a small cassette recorder to record the tour. Both methods afford the opportunity to express one's professionalism.

2. **Look at everything.** One must place himself or herself in the best possible position to render a judgment regarding the marketability and value of the property. This means becoming as familiar as possible with the entire property, which necessitates literally going through the house with a fine-tooth comb.

3. **Don't overreact.** While inspecting an owner's property, one must maintain a consistent demeanor. Many agents have the tendency to compliment the homeowners on their home with regard to choice of decor, condition, appearance, etc. This can be as damaging as reacting in a negative way to the owner's home. By overreacting to the home of the sellers, one reaffirms the sellers' belief that their home is truly

unique and worth more than it really is. In an effort to avoid this problem, one must not get carried away in telling the sellers what a great house it is, as such comments handicap the seller's receptiveness to pricing the property properly.

4. **Create an insecurity.** In addition to the preceding advantages, the agent should recognize that in order to create a receptive attitude in the seller to any aspect of utilizing an agent, the agent should attempt to tap the seller's insecurities about selling the property for as much as desired. Therefore, a little extra time should be spent in examining anything within the house that would affect its marketability in a negative way.

5. **Let them see that the agent sees everything.** While inspecting the property, one should bear in mind that every home has certain things wrong with it that the seller, as a result of living in the house every day, overlooks. Worns parts of carpet, spots on walls and ceilings, loose tiles in floors, etc., are all part of the normal wear and tear of a home. Each can often be unimportant but can also present a reason for suspicion on the part of the prospective purchaser with regard to the true condition of the property as well as the possible cost of correction. When locating one of these worn or soiled areas, merely running one's fingers across it or special scrutiny by the agent can cause these feelings of insecurity to surface within the homeowner. These feelings of insecurity often cause the homeowner to become more realistic about the property. (This should be done nonverbally unless there is a concern for possible structural damage or anything that would be corrected only following a major expenditure.)

During each part of the inspection, the agent should constantly be alert for similar areas of interest. Rapport often comes from aspects totally unrelated to real estate. The agent may notice pictures of little league teams in the boy's room; perhaps the agent has coached little league or has children who participated in little league. The same is true when noticing the "ego section" of the home. This section, represented by trophies, awards, etc., gives the agent an opportunity to discuss something other than the property.

No one has trophies or plaques on display unless proud of the achievement that earned them. Passing up a chance to get the customer into a conversation about these things is passing up the chance of adding to rapport.

Basically, one should always observe more than just the house in an effort to find an area on which one can relate to the customer other than business. Rapport is not something that comes free; one must work for it. Awareness can facilitate that job.

GETTING TO THE HEART OF THE PROBLEM

Once the home has been toured and carefully recorded notes have been made regarding the property, the agent must make a decision: "Can I successfully market this property within a reasonable period of time?" If the answer is yes, the agent must move from the fact-gathering posture into the fact-distributing posture, which allows one to establish an atmosphere in which the seller will be receptive to allowing the agent to present his or her opinions.

Note that I have said that the agent will have his or her opinions *heard* as opposed to *acted upon*. The reason is simple. If facts are presented properly, the proper action follows. If, however, one expects that an atmosphere for action exists, he or she is quite wrong. Only an atmosphere for listening exists; action comes as a result of what is presented. A fact-distributing posture is one designed to set the stage for the facts that must be considered. It is incumbent upon the REALTOR® to engage the seller in conversation regarding the marketing and sale of the property. Since the most obvious method for the disposal of the property would be through a REALTOR®, it is certainly fair to ask the seller the following.

> *Mr. (or Ms.) Seller, you have a very saleable house, if marketed properly, and I am curious why you have chosen to market your home without the services of a REALTOR®?*

Let's note what we have done. Before we can determine the direction of our presentation, we must determine the problems in the mind of the seller. We are merely asking why the seller has taken a specific course of action. In addition, we are letting the seller know that the house is in its most saleable position when it is marketed "properly" (i.e., with a REALTOR®).

An agent should never tell a seller that the property is saleable unless it is immediately qualified with "if marketed properly."

Nothing is saleable at the highest possible price unless it is marketed in the proper fashion. To make the statement that one has a very saleable property not only encourages the FSBO but also is an incomplete statement.

At this point, one of two responses will be forthcoming. Either the seller will express reasons for avoiding a REALTOR® or will prefer not to discuss it at all. Either response is advantageous for the agent. If the seller takes the former choice, then the agent has some insight as to the direction of the presentation. If, however, the seller chooses not to discuss the matter, then the agent can attempt to encourage the seller to reconsider. Rarely will the seller refuse to discuss the matter, but, when it happens, a simple question can free the topic for discussion. For example, the agent can ask

> *I understand how you feel, Mr. and Ms. Seller, but if I could show you a way of marketing your home differently than you are doing it now, without any of the problems or inconvenience, and net as much if not more money than you could net yourself, I'm sure you'd want to know about it, wouldn't you!*

In 99.9 percent of the cases the agent at this point will operate in an atmosphere for being heard. If however, the homeowner continues to refuse to discuss the situation, the agent has put himself or herself in a most influential position. He or she has viewed the property, met the sellers, established rapport, and made an attempt to cause the sellers to consider an alternative course of action. This was all done in a low-keyed fashion and is responsible for greater progress than could ever be made by a phone call. Should the agent view this question as to why the seller has chosen to market the home without the services of a REALTOR® as too direct in view of the telephone representation about not calling for a listing, there is an alternative.

> *Mr. and Ms. Seller, as I mentioned on the phone, I did want and appreciate the opportunity of seeing your property. After having seen the property, I feel it is saleable if marketed properly and I am curious as to why you have chosen not to utilize the services of a REALTOR®!*

This alternative acknowledges the earlier comment during the telephone conversation and, to some degree, softens the question of why they're not using a REALTOR®. This is unnecessary with most sellers because they are not threatened by such a simple question.

However, if the agent perceives such a problem, alternatives must be available.

Exercise

Using the direction suggested in this chapter, put together a dialogue for an agent to use in each of the three approaches to get appointments with FSBOs.

6

Structuring the
Listing Presentation

Having accomplished the first aspect of obtaining a listing—creating the atmosphere for communication—we must consider the proper structure of the presentation. There is no "one" proper way to make the presentation. There are any number. The only considerations are (1) Does the presentation address the areas of concern of the seller? (2) Is the agent comfortable with the presentation? Obviously, a well-designed and well-prepared presentation that fails to address the seller's concerns will fail, as will a presentation properly directed but lacking conviction on the part of the agent. Both ingredients are necessary.

APPROACH

There are basically two types of approaches that one can use in the pursuit of a listing: single appointment or multi-appointment. The single-appointment approach is an attempt to cover everything in one appointment, while the multi-appointment approach divides the listing presentation into modules, each with a specific purpose and objective.

Single-Appointment Approach

Obviously, if one is successful in obtaining the listing in one appointment, one could save an enormous amount of time. However, the real question is, can one be adequately competent and prepared to make a truly professional presentation in one interview? The probability is highly unlikely. Few listings are obtained during the first appointment. The reason is quite simple. Most sellers have questions that, to some degree, cannot be answered without some research by the agent—questions like, "How does my house compare to others that are on the market?" "Do the other houses in the neighborhood have the same features as my house?" "Two houses sold on the next block for $80,000 and mine is much nicer than they are, so doesn't that mean I can get more?"

Most of the time, the average agent is not prepared to answer these questions intelligently without first researching and preparing a visual that substantiates the position of the agent. Obviously, any agent can respond to any question, but the key is to respond in the most effective and professional manner. The most effective manner is when everything that one says is reinforced with written facts supporting one's responses.

If, however, one wishes to use the single-appointment approach, it is best used when in an area with similar construction, such as a tract development. In such an area, all the houses are very much alike.

During this presentation the agent utilizes all resources to overcome all apprehensions on the part of the seller to the listing at that time. The agent must inspect the property, build rapport with the seller, make the listing presentation, establish price and terms, and be prepared for any objections that the seller may have. This is a lot of pressure for the average agent.

Two-Appointment Process

In a listing presentation, much depends on what the agent senses should be done in terms of direction. Rather than my dictating the proper way to approach a situation, the agent should choose what he or she feels is best, as each situation is different.

Basically, this approach divides the entire presentation into two parts. It involves one appointment for the purpose of establishing an atmosphere for communication. Once this is achieved, the agent can go in one of two directions. The agent can proceed with a presentation of the benefits of a REALTOR®, benefits of the company, and why he or she is the best agent to handle the marketing of the property. The agent then can schedule a second appointment to meet the seller after the agent has had an opportunity to research the market and determine the best price at which to offer the property.

If preferred, however, the agent can reserve all discussion for the second appointment, with the first appointment purely a fact-gathering mission. The choice is entirely the agent's, as there are definite benefits to each approach. The ideal situation allows the agent to establish rapport during the first interview and, with the help of the seller, gather all the necessary measurements and data about the property in order to evaluate its position in the market properly. Following the collection of this information and while still in the seller's home, the agent schedules another appointment with the seller to review the results of the research.

This two-appointment approach should not be viewed as a delay in the presentation of the benefits of listing but rather as a logical progression allowing the seller to be in the best position to make the right decision. After all, this is an important decision. The more one tries to understand what the seller is going through and caters to those areas causing difficulties in making decisions, the more likely that one will be successful. The two-appointment process is merely an objective, not an absolute.

WHAT THE PRESENTATION SHOULD ACCOMPLISH

The presentation should show the seller how to accomplish his or her goals through the agent. Every seller has specific reasons for selling property. There are usually many things that he or she wishes to achieve with the proceeds from the sale of the home (a nicer home, new furniture, a vacation, etc.). If one can only listen beyond the words and find the best solution to the largest number of problems, one can often succeed where others have failed.

There are three primary objectives of every listing presentation. They are to show sellers: (1) why they need a REALTOR®, (2) why they need the agent's firm, and (3) why they need the agent.

Why the Seller Needs a REALTOR®

This is an extremely critical part of the listing presentation because it is here that the agent justifies the necessity of his or her assistance. Hardly a seller anywhere, regardless of how good a job a REALTOR® did for him or her, would admit that the REALTOR® was worth every penny charged. Too often we feel that if the sellers net what they want from the sale of their property, the amount of compensation paid to the REALTOR® is inconsequential. This is only partially true. If the sellers receive what they want from the sale of their home, they accomplish a tangible objective, but the REALTOR® often doesn't. The seller fails to recognize all that the REALTOR® has done on behalf of the seller in order to bring about that sale.

As a result of this lack of awareness on the part of the seller, few people appreciate the tremendous efforts of the REALTOR®. If this thought is challenged, I would ask the reader to locate a seller who had placed his or her property in the hands of any REALTOR® who ultimately sold the property in one day, with a REALTOR® fee of $10,000. This seller should be asked about the value that he or she placed on the services of that REALTOR®. Does he or she think that the REALTOR® was worth every penny received? Does he or she think that for this one day of marketing the property the REALTOR® was not worth $7,000 but rather the full $10,000?

With practically no exceptions, the response will be that though the seller is pleased with the quick sale and price, actually the fee for the REALTOR® was a bit extreme. The reason for this response *is not* that the REALTOR® was actually not worth the $10,000 fee, but rather, based on the limited knowledge that the seller has of what the REALTOR® actually does to market the property, this conclusion is drawn. A similar case is that of a couple who calls a REALTOR® to list their home and the REALTOR® fails to point out all that he or she is going to do for them (particularly what the sellers can't do for themselves). The obvious conclusion that the sellers draw is that they paid a lot of money for something that didn't require a great deal of effort or skill. These conclusions are logical deductions as a result of the limited input that the seller receives from the REALTOR®. Therefore, whose fault is it that such attitudes exist? It is the fault of the REALTOR®. If the agent is going to perpetuate his or her existence in the marketplace, he or she must get the message across to everyone, those who must be sold on the agent's services and those who are already sold.

While we could spend the next 50 pages on all the reasons for utilizing a REALTOR®, we must zero in on the most justifiable reasons . . . those that the sellers cannot do for themselves:

POINTS TO PONDER*

1. You have but one property to show; homes are bought by comparison.

*Reprinted from *real estate today®* by permission of the NATIONAL ASSOCIATION OF REALTORS®.

2. You do not know the tastes and requirements of the buyer, nor do you have first-hand knowledge of competitive values.

3. You do not know how to write a contract that is certain to be valid.

4. The buyer is timid about discussing his financial status with you and you are similarly reluctant.

5. You do not have time to leave your job to help arrange his financing, nor do you have expert knowledge on the current home loan market.

6. You cannot readily negotiate price with a buyer. But the third party, your REALTOR®, can work out the negotiations.

7. The average visitor will not admit freely to you his likes or dislikes, yet these must be brought into the open.

8. You cannot follow up, since this at once will be interpreted as your anxiety to sell in a hurry.

9. You may make needless outlays to improve your property for selling; the REALTOR®'s experience can save you needless expense.

10. You hear conflicting suggestions from well-meaning friends; we have answers from experience.

11. You may show your house to 100 would-be buyers; spend your time, money, and effort; and eventually pay a commission to a REALTOR® who properly screens prospective buyers.

12. You may accept an insincere offer and then spend months, perhaps, in litigation, to free your property in order to put it on the market once more.

13. You may find buyer's and seller's personalities conflict, thereby losing a good sale. The REALTOR®, as a third party, can diplomatically consummate the sale.

14. Most buyers seek the services of reputable REALTOR®s because they realize the pitfalls of direct negotiation.

15. The REALTOR® will enlist the services of fellow real estate people, giving the owner the advantage of the entire local sales market.

16. The REALTOR® will assist by furnishing current information regarding a fair market figure. The average owner overprices but eventually accepts a price below the market value.

From this group of 16 specific services the REALTOR® can provide that the sellers cannot, it is incumbent on each real estate agent to be able to call upon these when needed. One would not use all of these in each listing presentation. However, when the normal approach doesn't produce the listing, the agent needs alternatives. No matter what REALTOR® the sellers choose, they are better off with a REALTOR® as opposed to trying to sell their home themselves.

Why the Seller Needs the Agent's Company

Once the agent has accomplished the first part of the listing presentation's objectives, he or she proceeds to the second part, which is why the agent's company is the seller's best choice. This has been placed as the second aspect of the objectives rather than the first. Most agents attempt to persuade the seller to list based on the strengths of their companies. This is a major error in the beginning of a presentation because (1) it often fails to make the seller aware of all that the REALTOR® does in pursuing the sale of the seller's property and (2) with a for-sale-by-owner, it bypasses the sellers' main objection, the belief that they can sell it themselves.

Consequently, the advantages of one's company are expressed in vain, since the seller doesn't feel that he or she needs a REALTOR® at all. This approach usually results in responses from the seller such as "It sounds as though you have a great company, but we're just not ready to list" or "When we list we're going to list with you. Give us a couple of weeks and check back." It is the classic case of putting the cart before the horse. The discussion about the company must be reserved for the moment when the seller sees the advantages of dealing with a REALTOR®. At this juncture the seller is most receptive to the advantages of the agent's company.

Obviously, it is impossible to present all the advantages of dealing with one's company as opposed to any other company in the market. This information must be gathered from the management of the firm and presented in a logical and orderly sequence.

One very important rule is never knock the competition. In outlining the advantages of dealing with one's own company, the agent should do so without making a comparison to other specific companies but rather with the company's position in the market. Some areas to consider are:

- Location of the agent's office
- Age of the organization
- Size of the company
- Various internal supports (computer, membership in referral organizations producing out-of-town buyers, etc.)
- Areas of specialization
- Market share (percentage of the total activity in the marketplace for which the company is responsible)
- Annual volume (total, average per agent, and number of units)
- Background of principals in the company
- Company testimonial letters
- Community involvement
- Marketing plan

Location of Office

The easy accessibility of one's office is definitely an advantage in dealing with the company. Not only can the office staff show the property easily, but the agent can attract buyers interested in the area in which he or she is located.

Age of Organization

This is an advantage to both new and existing companies. The older company can expound upon its stability and its name recognition resulting from years in the business. The young company, on the other hand, can point out the fact that since it does not have the luxury of having been in business for x number of years, it will work harder to sell the sellers' property than anyone else. The young company is trying to establish itself and thus *needs* to sell the house more than others. Consequently, the agent will leave no stone unturned in the pursuit of this goal.

Size of the Company

The large company can play upon the strength of its size; more people are trying to sell the house. The smaller company, of course, can point out that big is not always best and that it believes in quality not quantity.

Internal Supports

All that a company does to make its operation run more smoothly and professionally should be mentioned to the seller. Many companies have some tie-in to a computer (either for their sole use or through MLS). Much time and money are spent by many companies in developing out-of-town referrals. This is done through the membership in referral organizations, participation in franchises, etc. This is a direct part of the company's personal advantages and should be shared with the seller.

Areas of Specialization

Companies specializing in residential real estate or in a specific area of the city have definite advantages to offer over those whose agents work all over town and also deal in commercial real estate. When dealing exclusively within one area, an agent is more likely to come across a buyer for the seller's home than one dealing in all areas. The same is true when dealing only with residential buyers as opposed to commercial buyers as well.

Market Share

To every seller the bottom line is always the results. Any company that can point out that it is responsible for a specific percentage of sales in a seller's area has a definite edge over the competition. The question is, What percentage of the market does the company have and how does that compare to other companies?

Annual Volume

People are impressed with figures. If the agent's company has done a record amount of business, it should be expressed to the sellers. No company does a lot of business consistently except by doing it right.

Background of Principals in Company

The better the image that one can project, the more positive the effect is on the public. Since the principals within the company are looked upon as an example for all within the company to follow and with the accepted axiom of like attracts like, the attributes of these people should be mentioned.

Company Testimonial Letters

Any time a client or customer takes the time to write a thank-you letter to a company for the fine job that it did, this letter should be exposed to potential clients and customers (after permission from the writer is obtained). Everyone likes to deal with a winner; third-party recommendations go a long way.

Community Involvement

When a company contributes to the community from which it gains its livelihood, people should be made aware of it. This strengthens the image of the company and helps position it as a responsible member of the community.

Marketing Plan

Every seller wants to know exactly what the agent is going to do to sell the property that makes him or her superior to others in the marketplace. This is the marketing plan. The agent must break each aspect of this plan into specific areas, and the sellers must be shown how each benefits them. Things such as advertising, open houses, availabilty of creative methods of financing, handling the sale from beginning to end, scheduling the showings, accountability to the seller and frequency, etc. (Basically one must gather this information from the broker, as each company is different).

Why the Seller Needs the Agent

This is a pivotal part of the presentation, because this is the reason for the ultimate decision to list. The agent must demonstrate to the sellers that he or she is the most professional, sincere, and responsible agent with whom to work. They must believe that the agent is knowledgeable. They must feel that the agent cares about their position and will truly work in their behalf. Usually, after showing the seller why they need a REALTOR® and why they need the agent's company, the agent has achieved most of this last aspect of the objectives of the presentation. However, having evidence to support this decision is a tremendous benefit. We will discuss this further when we talk about visual aids. Items such as copies of certificates from courses completed, testimonial letters, etc., are positive reinforcements.

FOUR PARTS OF THE PRESENTATION

There are four primary areas within each listing presentation. They are the opening, establishment of an understanding, benefits of listing, and listing close.

Step 1: Opening

Many agents have problems in bridging the gap between the inspection of the property and the discussion of the listing. The opening serves as this bridge. Since the agent wants to determine as quickly as possible the direction that must be taken in order to address the problems of the seller, in the opening one can get an indication for this and progress into the discussion of listing at the same time. The following suggestion, put into the agent's own words, accomplishes this:

> Mr. and Ms. Seller, may I ask why you have chosen to market the home without the services of a REALTOR®?
> or
> Mr. and Ms. Seller, I feel that you have a very saleable home if marketed properly, and I am curious as to why you have chosen to do so without the services of a REALTOR®.

That opening is for dealing with a FSBO. With the seller who has invited you to the home to get an idea of what you have to offer, the opening is much more direct.

> Mr. and Ms. Seller, I appreciate very much your giving me the opportunity to tell you about our marketing program and how it will benefit you if we are given the responsibility of marketing your home.

From this brief opening the agent moves, as from each of the other openings, directly into the second part of the presentation.

Step 2: Establishment of an Understanding

In the case of the FSBO, this step is covered to a greater degree than in the case of a seller who is just trying to decide on which REALTOR®. With the FSBO, the idea is to communicate this thought:

> Mr. and Ms. Seller, if I could show you a way to market your home differently from the way you are doing it now, with none of the problems or inconveniences, and net as much if not more money than you could net yourself, you'd want to know about it wouldn't you?

This line of questioning is designed to get an affirmative response so that the FSBO is receptive to the advantages or at least listens with an open mind. Should the FSBO respond negatively, this negates the earlier assumption that he or she will listen to the agent, based on the response to step 1. Therefore, one must discover why the FSBO is not receptive to an alternative that would be the best of all worlds. Unless the FSBO will listen, the agent accomplishes nothing. When the customer patronizes the agent and listens with unspoken objections, the agent is doing himself or herself more harm than good in ignoring this.

In the case of the seller who is receptive to listing but not sure with whom, this step is briefer, as a result of the obvious openness to listen. With this individual one might cover this step by communicating the thought "Mr and Ms. Seller, our objective is to sell your house for the greatest amount of money in the shortest possible time. These are the reasons we think we can do just that." This simple comment gets the seller's attention; one immediately moves to the third part of the presentation.

Step 3: Sell the Benefits

In this aspect of the presentation, the agent has the resonsibility of discussing the three objectives of the presentation (why use a REALTOR®, why use the company, and why use the agent). The approach that we take depends on the direction that we sense the seller needs us to take. How one does this depends upon the creativeness of the agent and the awareness of the agent as to the seller's motives.

Step 4: Closing the Listing

Once all points have been discussed, and the seller has expressed (either verbally or nonverbally) an understanding and agreement with the points discussed, one must get the signature on the listing agreement. What brings about this action on the part of the seller is called *closing the listing.*

THE LISTING PRESENTATION

Step 1

AGENT: *Mr. (or Ms.) Jones, after looking at your home, I feel that it is very saleable if marketed properly. May I ask you why you have chosen to market it without the services of a REALTOR®?*

HOMEOWNER: *We want to try it ourselves.*

Step 2

AGENT: *I can certainly appreciate that you feel that way, but if I could show you how you could market your home differently than you are doing it now and net as much money, if not more, than you could net yourself, you'd want to know about it, wouldn't you?*

HOMEOWNER: *Yes, if that is possible.*

Step 3

AGENT: *Mr. (or Ms.) Jones, the marketing of any real estate is at best difficult. Today homes are bought by comparison. You have only one property to show and must depend on the buyer to go out, look at other homes, and then come back to yours. This is certainly a disadvantage, isn't it?*

HOMEOWNER: *Yes, it's difficult, but for 6 percent of the sale price, I don't mind difficulties.*

AGENT: *You're right! A few difficulties are surely worth the REALTOR®'s commission, if you could net as much. The problem is that most FSBO shoppers know that the only reason a homeowner is selling the home that way is to save the commission; the first thing they do is knock the commission off the price of the house, because the buyer is interested in saving the commission as well. When two people are trying to get the same thing, somebody has to lose; unfortunately, it is usually the seller. Besides, the only thing you're really concerned with is the net dollars to you, aren't you?*

HOMEOWNER: *Which is exactly why we've decided to sell it ourselves, so we can net more.*

AGENT: *Of course, but with the buyer after the commission, the reality of that taking place is somewhat remote, isn't it?*

HOMEOWNER: *What makes you think that you can net us more?*

AGENT: *Because of all the services we can provide so that we can reach more buyers. I'm sure you'll agree that with the multiple-listing service, which ties us in to all the local real estate salespeople, the odds of our reaching the right buyer for your home are certainly greater than yours might be, aren't they?*

HOMEOWNER: *Yes, I guess so.*

AGENT: *That is the very reason why we can probably net you as much, if not more, money than you could net yourself. You see, the law of supply and demand tells us that the more people to whom we have to sell something, the higher the price. The fewer people to sell something to, the lower the price. Because of the limited exposure that an owner can give a home, the available buyers are few in number, which means a lower price. Now, of course, you don't have to sell for a lower price, but that's not what really matters. What really matters is selling your home for the highest possible net dollars to you, isn't it?*

HOMEOWNER: *Absolutely!*

AGENT: *If we can agree on a price that will net you what you want, would you be willing to market your home with our company?*

HOMEOWNER: *If we can agree.*

AGENT: *Let's first take a look at what you need to net from the sale of your property. How much is that?*

HOMEOWNER: *$50,000.*

AGENT: *And what is the balance of your mortgage?*

HOMEOWNER: *About $50,000.*

AGENT: *(Recognizing that $100,000 net to the seller would price the house out of the market and that the true value of the home is probably $95,000 to $97,000, the agent tactfully proceeds.) The $50,000 net that you mentioned is what you would use to pay all related costs of selling, with the exception of the commission, isn't it?*

Homeowner: *Yes, we could do that, but not your commission.*

AGENT: *Let me ask you this. If someone looked at your house and offered you a price for your property that would mean $40,000 cash in your pocket, you give possession when it is convenient, and have no problems before closing, what would you do?*

HOMEOWNER: *Do you have such a buyer?*

AGENT: *If I did, what would you do?*

HOMEOWNER: *We'd sell.*

Step 4

AGENT: *(Handing the seller a Net Sheet showing approximate net dollars) You'll be delighted to know that at a listed price of $97,000, we can net you just that amount and perhaps a little more! Would you like me to put your ad in the* Post *or the* Chronicle?

HOMEOWNER: *Whichever one will produce that buyer.*

GET THE SELLER INVOLVED

As evident throughout the preceding example, one must keep the seller involved. The conversation with the seller must be just that, a conversation. One must avoid doing all the talking. Every time a point is made, it must be followed with comments such as "I'm sure you can see how this is to your advantage, can't you?" or "This is in the direction you wanted, isn't it?"

There must be a confirmation on the part of the seller not only of understanding but also agreeing with the various points of the presentation. If one allows an area of disagreement or misunderstanding to pass without being aired, one will only hinder further points of importance within the presentation.

VISUAL AIDS

The most professional method of selling is with the use of visual aids. Although this is a technique that the majority of real estate salespeople resist the most, it is unquestionably the direction that all must ultimately go in order to survive the revolution that sales is experiencing.

The best evidence of the direction that salespeople must pursue is indicated by the most professional sales organizations. Unfortunately, the real estate industry has always compared itself to others in its ranks in order to determine its degree of professionalism. To stay ahead of the competition is certainly necessary, but in the long run to keep up with the professional salespeople with whom the customers deal is the real test. Many homeowners, through their work, deal with salespeople representing the most professional and best-equipped sales organizations. If an agent expects to gain the trust and confidence of customers and clients, he or she must adopt the traits of these other salespeople. Visual aids are · consistent with those characteristics. Specifically, a presentation manual is a means of giving visual support to the representations which one is making to one's customers and clients.

Presentation Manual

People believe what is written infinitely faster than what they are told. In addition, the adult's attention span is very short; unless one takes care to hold the customer's attention, the mind wanders. From the agent's perspective, one can lose continuity and flow in the presentation as a result of the numerous directions of the customer's conversation during the listing interview.

For all these reasons, the agent must have a means of circumventing these obstacles to the sale. The use of a presentation manual accomplishes this objective.

Advantages of a Presentation Manual

1. Building of credibility. Any time a customer can review, in writing, supporting evidence to what is presented, he or she will more easily accept and trust the salesperson. The agent must incorporate this in the presentation. The agent always furnishes some things in writing (i.e., mortgage information, appraisal data, listing and sales agreements, etc.) but should consider going beyond these points, putting as much of the presentation as possible in some written form.

2. Professional characteristic. A presentation manual is a typical characteristic of the finest salespeople. As mentioned, real estate agents must adopt the characteristics of the salespeople with whom most of our customers are in contact, from top-flight, high-powered sales organizations. If one were to invite such salespersons to present their products, an interesting consistency would present itself; they would probably all use presentation manuals. These com-

panies all recognize the necessity of such sales aids, and they take advantage of this knowledge.

3. Attention-holder. We have discussed the problems with adult's short attention span. Also we are capable of thinking faster than we can talk, approximately four times the rate of speech. It only makes sense that the salesperson utilize something to overcome this barrier in communicating.

4. Orderly Sequence. In view of the frequent changes in direction during a presentation in a listing interview, coupled with the agent's need to remain flexible and go whatever direction that the customer takes, the agent can often be frustrated and confused. The agent frequently is unable to return to the point being made before the customer has caused a deviation from the planned presentation. The agent's only alternative is to make the best of it and attempt to proceed in some logical and intelligent progression. This is, to say the least, difficult. There is hardly a real estate agent to be found who has not left a listing appointment realizing that he or she failed to mention something or that a portion of the ordinary presentation had been omitted. This is inevitable unless there is some visual way to remind oneself of what one wishes to say, such as a presentation manual.

Each of the advantages in using a presentation manual becomes a real disadvantage for the agent who opts not to use one. This is another area in which the agent has a choice. The agent either can avoid these problems by using a presentation manual or can continually deal with them because of not using one.

Developing a Presentation Manual

In creating a presentation manual, there are some very important factors to keep in mind. First, the agent should not use, in its entirety, someone else's manual. The presentation manual must be personalized in order to be effective; it must be a reflection of the agent. One should take ideas from everyone but make sure that the manual is personalized. Second, the agent should jot down the areas that he or she prefers to emphasize during most appointments. The agent can come up with a rough outline of the presentation. Naturally, one can't think of everything that ordinarily will be discussed with sellers, but the agent can come up with all the things that he or she wants to mention to every seller.

Let's examine more closely the second point. One could jot down areas to emphasize during a listing presentation. This list would be in no specific order in terms of when the items will be mentioned, but is rather a random list. The agent must then take each item and break it into specifics about each area.

Example

1. Reasons for using a REALTOR®:

- You have but one property to show; homes are bought by comparison.
- The average visitor will not admit freely to you his likes or dislikes, yet these must be brought into the open.
- You cannot follow up, since this at once will be interpreted as your anxiety to sell in a hurry.
- You may accept an insincere offer and then spend months, perhaps, in litigation, to free your property in order to put it on the market once more.

2. Reasons for using the company:

- Average annual expenditure by company for procuring out-of-town buyers (cost of trips, mailings, printing of materials, entertaining corporation executives, etc.)
- Annual advertising budget
- List of publications in which firm advertises
- Open houses
- Creative financing alternatives
- Accountability to seller
- Size of the organization
- Number of offices
- Years of service, total and average, of agents in real estate and with company

STRUCTURING THE LISTING PRESENTATION   81

- Office's special projects in the community
- Positions held by principals and fellow agents within real estate organizations

3. Reasons for using the agent

- Personal activity in the area
- Certificates of course work
- Testimonials
- Newspaper clippings

This list is in no way as complete as one developed after deliberations on each area. This chapter does not give the reader a presentation manual but rather causes one to think about presentation manuals and their content in order to develop one that is unique.

If we were to develop individual visuals supporting each point on the list, we might do so in the following manner.

1. "You have only one home to show and today homes are bought by comparison." The agent should show a visual with customer telling salesperson, "Based on the four other homes we've seen, this certainly is the finest value . . . we'll take it!"

2. "The average visitor will not admit freely to you his likes or dislikes, yet these must be brought into the open." The agent shows a visual with a couple leaving a house; half showing buyers telling the seller how much they love it and the other, buyers outside telling each other how ugly the carpet was.

3. "You cannot follow up, since this at once will be interpreted as your anxiety to sell in a hurry." The agent has a visual showing a seller calling a buyer and the buyer indicating to spouse, "This guy must be in a hurry. Maybe we can get a better price."

4. Size of organization. Photo of sales staff.

5. Years of service. Capital letters: *OVER 100 YEARS OF EXPERIENCE.*

6. Positions held by principals or other agents. Ms. Jane Phillips of ABC Realty, current president of local board of REALTOR®s.

7. Personal activity in area. List of homes with agent's personal involvement in selling.
8. Certificates. Certificates of completion of real estate courses and other designations.
9. Testimonials. Copies of testimonials.
10. Newspaper clippings. Copies of clippings showing agent as agent of month/year.

At this point, the agent has several pages with which to begin a presentation manual. One must assemble the pages in the order best fitting the flow of the presentation and practice turning the pages with the presentation. Using the manual soon becomes second nature. It is best to put the manual in a two- or three-ring binder and have each of the pages encased in plastic for long life.

Anyone who has ever played golf or tennis and then decided to take lessons experiences the same kind of initial discomfort felt when beginning to use a presentation manual. Just as with tennis and golf lessons, ultimately one learns to use the manual better and more effectively.

The effectiveness and ease with which one learns to use a presentation manual will be absolutely amazing. There will be constant improvements to the manual as time passes. This results from discovering new and different aspects to emphasize. In time the agent will become as strong an advocate of the manual as I am and will never again make a listing presentation without it. The agent will realize that he or she is more effective at obtaining listings than ever before.

COMPETITIVE MARKET ANALYSIS

The introduction of this form (Figure 6-1) is unusually effective in the pursuit of listings (and sales). It is a simple form that draws a comparison between a seller's property and other properties that are similar and (1) have sold, (2) are for sale, and (3) have been on the market and did not sell. It takes into consideration buyer appeal and financial position of the property and breaks down the seller's cost of selling the property. It should be completed and used in all listing presentations (the one featured in Figure 6-1 is available through the REALTOR®s National Marketing Institute, 430 North Michigan Avenue, Chicago, Illinois 60611). Most multiple-listing services have the information which one would use in the preparation of this form.

The obvious strength of this form is that it shows the seller how to approach logically the correct price at which the house should be offered to the public. Using these approaches to value (what has sold, what is for sale, and what did not sell) not only will the agent more professionally advise the seller as to price but will also be correct more frequently.

Exercise

Prepare your idea of a presentation manual, utilizing some ideas mentioned in this chapter and no less than five ideas of your own.

Property Address _____ Date _____

For Sale Now:	Bed-rms.	Baths	Den	Sq. Ft.	1st Loan	List Price	Days on Market	Terms

Sold Past 12 Mos.	Bed-rms.	Baths	Den	Sq. Ft.	1st Loan	List Price	Days on Market	Date Sold	Sale Price	Terms

Expired Past 12 Mos.	Bed-rms.	Baths	Den	Sq.Ft.	1st Loan	List Price	Days on Market	Terms

F.H.A.—V.A. Appraisals

Address	Appraisal	Address	Appraisal

84

Buyer Appeal

Marketing Position

(Grade each item 0 to 20% on the basis of desirability or urgency)

1 Fine Location _____ %	1 Why Are They Selling _____ %
2 Exciting Extras _____ %	2 How Soon Must They Sell _____ %
3 Extra Special Financing _____ %	3 Will They Help Finance ....Yes ____ No ____ %
4 Exceptional Appeal _____ %	4 Will They List at Competitive Market Value ....Yes ____ No ____ %
5 Under Market Price ____ Yes ____ No ____ %	5 Will They Pay for Appraisal ....Yes ____ No ____ %
Rating Total _____	Rating Total _____

Assets _____

Drawbacks _____

Area Market Conditions _____

Recommended Terms _____

Selling Costs	
Brokerage	$
Loan Payoff	$
Prepayment Privilege	$
FHA — VA Points	$
Title and Escrow Fees: IRS Stamps, Recons. Recording	$
Termite Clearance	$
Misc. Payoffs: 2nd T. D., Pool, Patio, Water Softener, Fence, Improvement Bond	$
	$
	$
	$
Total	$

Top Competitive Market Value $ _____

Probable Final Sales Price $ _____

Total Selling Costs $ _____

Net Proceeds $ _____ Plus or Minus $ _____

The statements and figures presented herein, while not guaranteed, are secured from sources we believe authoritative.

Prepared by _____

FIGURE 6-1. Competitive Market Analysis

7

Handling Sales Resistance

Most salespeople are terrified of being confronted with the most obvious form of sales resistance, an objection. When such a barrier occurs, the salesperson must attempt to show the client why that objection is not as great a problem as he or she sees it. If one were certain that what was being proposed was in fact right for the client, the objection would not be a problem. If, however, the salesperson is somewhat unsure that what he or she is selling is really in the best interests of the client, the salesperson naturally experiences great anxieties. These anxieties cause tremendous discomfort in dealing with sales resistance. By eliminating the cause of the anxiety, one eliminates the problem entirely. Therefore, one must be certain that he or she is in a position to reach the conclusion that the customer does in fact need the service that he or she is offering. This level of understanding can only come with a probing and complete listing interview.

WHAT OBJECTIONS MEAN

People never bring up objections unless they like the item or service being offered. If one were to analyze what occurs when an objection is expressed, one would discover that the area of concern is the only negative in the mind of the customer. If someone doesn't like an item or service being offered, the person would reject it in its entirety and not isolate the objection to one or two specific areas. The response would be a simple, "No, thank you, I don't think we'll be interested in listing." That would be the end. Fortunately, the customer will generally mention particular areas of concern, such as the length of the listing, the amount of the commission, etc. When this occurs, the customer is saying, "Tell me how I can live with the term of your listing." or "Show me why I should list in spite of your fee."

In other words, "Everything looks fine, but there is one area of which I'm not certain." This is not the usual route taken by most salespeople. Most of the time the average salesperson interprets any objection as an absolute rejection of the listing and ceases any further effort.

OBJECTIONS COME IN TWO FORMS

Basically, there are two forms of objections: (1) an objection for the sake of objecting and (2) an objection to a condition. Objections for the sake of objecting are more frequent than any other. This objection stems from sales resistance and is an unconscious attempt by the individual to avoid being sold. The person doesn't have any specifics for objections and comes up with something without substance. A good example is when the sellers, after expressing their need to sell as soon as possible due to an out-of-town transfer and wanting to show the house to everyone possible, say, "We're going to stay as a for-sale-by-owner because if we list, we'll have to have the house ready to show at all times." Based on the knowledge regarding the seller's urgency to sell, this objection is probably invalid. There can always be extenuating circumstances causing this response, but in normal cases this is an objection for the sake of objecting.

Objections to a condition are an entirely different matter. Such an objection can rarely be overcome. Such would be the case of a party whose objection was "I'm afraid we can't list now due to the fact that we have some title problems." This objection obviously presents a condition prohibiting the transfer of the title to the property. Unless this condition can be overcome — which may require an attorney — pursuing the listing could be an exercise in futility.

In view of these types of objections, the agent must be aware of the circumstances surrounding the sellers' need to sell, in an effort to determine the true validity of the objections. In any case, objections by the customer are a good sign. People never object to anything specifically unless they like the idea generally.

FIVE EASY STEPS FOR OVERCOMING OBJECTIONS

Before we begin to deal with specific objections raised on a listing appointment, we must establish some structure to follow in the process of dealing with sellers and their objections. The steps are: (1) listen attentively, (2) acknowledge the customer's point of view, (3) qualify the objection, (4) answer the objection, and (5) close.

1. *Listen attentively.* This step is simple but important. The client must realize that the agent is listening to every word and that the objection is considered important.

2. *Acknowledge the seller's point of view.* Uninformed sellers will raise many objections. While they believe that their objections are sound, the fact that they are based on improper information invalidates their position. The worst thing that a salesperson can do, however, is to flaunt the seller's error in attempt to show how right the agent is. If this ever occurs and the agent takes this inappropriate approach in dealing with it, at best the customer will politely refuse to list with the agent. Anytime an agent does anything threatening the self-image of a client, the agent loses.

   In acknowledging the viewpoint of the seller, the agent merely says, "I can appreciate how you feel, however . . . " or "I understand your concern, but . . . ." By utilizing this technique, the agent is telling the seller that how he or she feels is understandable and the seller has every right to feel that way; however, perhaps there are some new developments or additional bits of information to consider. This is not only a gentler way of approaching an area about which the customer must be corrected but also far more tactful.

3. *Qualify the objection.* Before dealing with any objection, the agent must be sure that there are no others. If there are, one must attempt to have all the objections expressed before dealing with any of them. This can be achieved through a line of questioning that says something to the effect of "If you weren't concerned about _____ , then in your opinion do you feel that you would want to market your property with our firm?"

This question can obviously be answered *yes* or *no*. If the answer is *yes*, the agent knows that all he or she must do is overcome the single objection and proceed to step 4. If the response is *no*, the agent knows immediately that the customer sees another problem. In this case, the agent proceeds to the second part of step 3, finding out why. This is done by inquiring as to the reason that the customer feels the way he or she does. The agent may ask, "Mr. _____, I am sure you have some reason for feeling that way; may I ask what it is?" At this point the customer will express the other areas of concern. Then all objections must be qualified ("I see, so if it weren't for _____ , _____ , and _____ , you would have already listed your home, wouldn't you?"). Upon receiving a positive response to step 3, either on the initial attempt or after having qualified all their objections, the agent can proceed to step 4.

4. *Answer the objection.* In this step we offer all the necessary reasons that put the client's fears to rest. (Later we discuss exactly how we might deal with specific objections, but first we must learn the structure for dealing with objections.)

5. *Close.* It is at this point that the salesperson has heard the objection, acknowledged the seller's position, qualified the objection, answered it, and must now offer a suggestion causing the seller to make the decision to list.

In the following example of the application of the five-step process, the reader should try to identify the use of each step:

OBJECTION: *I am in the advertising business and can run ads that will produce just a many buyers as your ads will.*

AGENT: *I can appreciate how you feel, Mr. Seller, and if it weren't for your expertise in advertising, I suspect that you would market your house with me this evening, wouldn't you?*

SELLER: *Yes.*

AGENT: *The interesting aspect of marketing resi-*

dential real estate, Mr. Seller, is that advertising contributes to a very small percentage of sales. Our experience has been that less than 11 percent of our business results from advertising and that the vast majority of our sales actually comes from the contacts and promoting in which our company is engaged. For instance, we are a member of a large nationwide referral network, involving REALTOR®s all over the country. When any of our members have customers moving to our city, we are the REALTOR® contacted. I am sure that you can see what a tremendous advantage this is, can't you?

SELLER: *I had no idea that you had marketing efforts of this type.*

AGENT: *Yes, and we are ready to put them to work for you. Would you prefer that we put our sign up this evening or wait until morning?*

SELLER: *Let's get started right away.*

HOW TO HANDLE TYPICAL OBJECTIONS

In this section I am going to attempt to answer many of the objections to listing confronting an agent during a career in real estate. These are not the only ways to deal with these objections, nor will they always succeed. They are, in fact, logical methods of overcoming barriers. The agent must be certain that all suggestions are compatible with the goals and policies of his or her company and that state laws are not infringed. I am not going to use the five-step approach with each objection, but merely share possible answers.

Objection 1: *We have a friend in the business.*

This kind of objection is not of any great consequence but many times can cripple the agent. These people probably have more than one friend in the real estate business, in which case, once this fact has been established, an appropriate response might be:

AGENT: *As I see it, Mr. Seller, you will have a problem in deciding which friend with whom to market your house, won't you?*

SELLER: *(Positive Response)*

AGENT: *Perhaps the best thing for you to do is not to list with any of your friends. In view of the magnitude of this investment (the home), it is in your best interest to have someone handle the sale of your property with whom you don't have to stand on ceremony. Often this is hard to achieve with a friend. If you list your home with me, you can tell your friends that since you had more than one friend in real estate, you decided to deal with an outside party.*

The agent must, through the use of visuals (testimonials, sales records, etc.), show the seller that he or she is the most dominant REALTOR® in the area, based on the fact that last year the firm was responsible for x percent of the sales in the sellers' subdivision. "Surely, Ms. Seller, you do want to market your home with a company with a high success record in your area, don't you?"

When none of the preceding reasons are sufficient and the concern for the sellers' friend is so great that in spite of the agent's outstanding record and obvious ability to bring about the quickest sale, they wish to use their friend, the agent must consider a minor concession. He or she must determine if the concern on the part of the sellers is because of a loyalty to the friend stemming from the sellers' belief that the friend can do a better job, or if it is because of the sellers' desire to see that the friend earns something from the sale. Usually, the sellers want to have their friend benefit from the commission. In this situation, this might be in order:

AGENT: *Mr. Seller, as I see it your main concern is to have your friend participate in the commission from the sale of your property, is that right?*

SELLER: *(Positive Response)*

AGENT: *In that case, let me offer you a solution. I will be happy to execute a letter to your friend obligating our firm to pay to his company x percent of the commission that we receive from the sale of your property in the form of a referral fee. This fee will be paid as our gesture of good faith on your behalf and will require nothing on their part. How does that sound?*

The agent must not, of course, obligate the company to pay more than the standard referral fee. Though the friend did not actually make the referral, if this is the only way to get the listing, isn't it worth it? This is offered only as a last resort.

Objection 2: *We have someone who's interested and we want to wait and see what they are going to do.*

This is obviously a valid concern on the part of any seller. The agent must approach this carefully so as not to appear high pressure. The best approach is to determine how long the seller wishes to wait for this buyer's decision. Once this is determined, there are two directions to take.

1. The agent can ask the seller to market the home with him or her and reserve the name of the buyer for the time that the seller had wanted to wait for this person's decision.

2. The agent can ask the seller for a postdated listing, which would not commence until the seller feels the buyer will have reached a decision.

Naturally, one would rather have the sellers forget about that buyer and list the property immediately, but this is not always practical. There must be some alternative in this situation. The reserving of a buyer's name simply protects the seller from having to pay a commission to the REALTOR® should the seller sell the property to the buyer in question, providing the sale occurs within the stipulated time frame.

Objection 3: *We'll give you a listing for 30 days.*

This is a common objection, in that the seller wants to cut down the listing period. The logical approach to this is to point out that in order to get top price for the property, the amount of time to market the property must be adequate to locate the best buyer. This is only achieved when the market has been thoroughly searched; that search takes time. The best support for the length of a listing is showing the seller the average length of time to bring about sales on the properties in the area. These facts are usually available from the local MLS. When a seller sees in black and white that the average time to market property in the area has been x number of days, it is logical that he or she must expect to allow a comparable amount of time.

Objection 4: *We don't want to pay a commission.*

When this type of objection is raised, an effective response is:

I don't blame you, Ms. Seller, but the most important result to you is the amount of net dollars you receive from the sale of your home, isn't it?

At this point it is important to show the seller what other homes in the area have sold for (if already done, the agent must show them again) and point out that they sold as a result of the efforts of the REALTOR®. It is important to address the approaches that the company takes to attract buyers and the expense that it incurs in the process. This is another advantage of dealing with the REALTOR® that the seller is unable to provide on his or her own.

Another alternative is to point out what affects the ultimate sale price. This is, of course, exposure to the marketplace. Approximately 95 percent of the buyers seek the services of reputable REALTOR®s, which leaves approximately 5 percent who will go directly to the seller. Being able to expose the property to 19 times as many buyers as the seller can, the REALTOR® is in a better position to locate the buyer who will pay the greatest amount for the property.

The law of supply and demand dictates that the more people there are to sell something to, the higher the price; the fewer people to sell something to, the lower the price. This applies with the greatest significance to the decision to sell without a REALTOR® versus with a REALTOR®. Selling the property without a REALTOR® severely narrows the available market. As the market narrows, so does the possibility of locating the best buyers who will pay the most.

What is meant by the *best* buyer? The *best buyer* is someone who has a specific desire to own a home with all the advantages and conveniences of the seller's home. This buyer will pay more for this home than someone who wants a home with the same number of bedrooms as the seller's home but is interested in little else. Therefore, if one is going to sell, one wants to sell to the best buyer. Locating this buyer is not an easy job. It takes a full-time effort of an entire company to succeed; for this reason the seller is doing an injustice to himself or herself as well as the family by not using a REALTOR®. The seller is, of course, free to sell to anyone, but *selling* the home is not the secret. The secret is to sell to the best buyer. When this results, everyone wins—seller, buyer, and REALTOR®. Unfortunately, due to the lack of conviction on the part of many REALTOR®s on this point, FSBOs continue.

Objection 5:   *Another company said that they will charge less commission.*

Agents frequently respond to this objection with one of these responses.

Every company is free to charge whatever it feels its services are worth.

or

Every company charges in direct proportion to the value they place on their services.

These statements are very true, but the agent needs to expound upon the fact that the services offered can only be provided if the company can make a profit. Making a profit cannot be obtained at a low commission rate; consequently, what the REALTOR® can do for the homeowner is impaired. The most important result is net dollars. It doesn't matter what one's commission rate is if the sellers can net what they want from the sale. In most cases the difference in what the other company has agreed to charge is not enough of a difference to keep the house from selling when added to the price of the house.

Another factor is that the seller has not yet listed with this other company at the lower commission rate, so there is something about which the seller is not yet clear. The agent must stress what he or she can do and direct the seller's attention to the net dollars, not spend time discussing commission dollars.

Objection 6: *We'll pay you the amount of fee that you'd receive if you were selling another company's listing.*

This is treated in much the same way as the attempt to get the REALTOR® to cut the fee. Net dollars are all that matter and if the seller nets what he or she wants, the amount of the REALTOR®s' fee is inconsequential.

Objection 7: *I have a license (or I'm an attorney) and want part of the commission.*

In this case, the individual has the legal right to participate in the commission, but not necessarily the moral right. It is not wise to raise this moral issue to individuals attempting to be included in the commission because they probably don't care. This does not mean that they are immoral people, only that they have probably worked it out in their minds that they should receive part of the commission. The "moral" aspect will most probably cause friction.

One must determine if they are firm about a share of the commission by trying to show that if they net what they want, the commission is negligible. If, however, they are firm on participating in the commission, one must ascertain to what extent. If their desired portion is not unreasonable—and sometimes if it is—the agent should try to add it to the sale price of the house and get the full commission. If, however, this is not practical due to the high price of the house, the agent should consider offering a referral fee as a token of good faith. This referral fee should not, of course, be more than the company is willing to pay. If the referral fee is not enough for the individual and all else has failed, the agent must make a decision, best reached with input from management. This decision is whether to take the listing and pay the sellers the portion that they want or to reject the listing. Neither decision is easy; in certain situations, either will prove correct.

Objection 8:   *I've been in sales all my life and I can sell this house myself.*

In this situation, the agent must be careful not to say anything threatening the self-image of the seller. The agent's approach should be to agree that it is the seller's right to sell the home. However, showing the house is not the important aspect of the sale. What is important is locating the best buyer for the property, which is the agent's primary objective.

Taking this position, the agent acknowledges the sales ability of the seller and focuses attention on what the agent can do that the seller cannot.

Objection 9:   *I dealt with a REALTOR® once and will never do it again.*

Bad experiences are part of everyone's past. A bad experience tends to stay with one for a long time. The best approach to this kind of an objection is to point out to the seller that there are always people who do not demonstrate the competence level of a profession, but this does not mean that all members of that profession subscribe to the same set of standards. Many times this is best achieved by drawing an analogy with the seller's profession or business.

AGENT: *Mr. Jones, you mentioned that you and your wife are both accountants, didn't you?*

SELLER: *(Positive response)*

AGENT: *I am sure that you are both very good at what you do, aren't you?*

SELLER: *(Positive response)*

AGENT: *Unfortunately, there are probably accountants whose ap-*

                   proach to public accounting is a disgrace to the profession, wouldn't you agree!

SELLER: *(Positive response)*

AGENT: *Mr. Jones, just as those people are not reasons for your customers to start doing their own accounting and not using you, your experience is not necessarily a reason to judge all REALTOR®s by the actions of one, is it!*

Objection 10:   *We want to get a higher price than you are suggesting.*

This objection has many hidden meanings, none impossible for the agent to overcome, if only by considering the seller's background. When a seller says anything that indicates that he or she wants a higher price than reasonably expected, the agent must immediately take a course of action to arm the seller with the same information that led the agent to the recommended price. First, no one can get a price for anything that is not in line with the market unless one makes concessions (i.e., carry a second mortgage, etc.). Rather than debate about why the agent is right and that wanting more is unreasonable, one must give some data so that the seller can see the agent's point of view and thus be won over.

For instance, if sellers say that they want $97,500 for their $80,000 house, the agent must ask how they arrived at that price. If they used nothing other than *instinct* to reach their decision, the agent should share with them the current sales and listings in the neighborhood, as well as those houses not selling, in order to allow them to conclude on their own that their price is unreasonable. Sellers are smart. If only they are privileged to the same information as the REALTOR®, they will logically follow the same route as the REALTOR® and reach similar conclusions.

When sellers question the logical price in spite of the other houses on the market, the agent has no alternative but to show them houses competing with their house. After seeing houses that are obviously better investments than theirs, the agent should ask the simple question, "Mr. Jones, if you were looking for a home such as this and you looked at this home at the price being offered and your home at the price you are suggesting, in which house would you invest?" The answer is obvious. The seller is led to a decision based on understandable and logical reasoning.

An alternative might be to approach the listing with the idea that the sellers might need input from an outside party, such as an appraiser. The approach establishes with the sellers that certainly they would not want their home on the market at a figure less than it's worth and neither would they want the house on the market at a figure too high, with their house then being shown by agents as a reason for a buyer to invest in something else. One can proceed with the idea that since the sellers think that they are correct in their price and the agent thinks that he or she is correct in the price, a fee appraiser (of the sellers' choosing) should appraise the house.

If the appraiser's figure is closer to the sellers' price than the REALTOR®'s price, the agent will pay for the appraisal. However, if the appraiser appraises the house at a figure closer to the REALTOR®'s price than to the sellers' price, the sellers will pay for it.

This is an extremely good technique in bringing sellers back to reality. Usually they will put more validity in the agent's figures as a result of such willingness to "put your money where your mouth is." If, however, they choose to have the appraisal, the agent is almost assured of the listing. The appraiser will use the same information that the agent did to arrive at the price. If the agent has not prepared properly, the appraiser may well have a dramatically different price, in which case the agent must pay for the appraisal.

If the appraisal is closer to the sellers' figure than to the agent's, one must not feel defeated. Everyone is human; every agent will make mistakes. The appropriate action at this point is to examine the appraiser's figures and determine that the comparable properties used by the appraiser are in fact appropriate. Upon concurring with the appraiser, the agent must convey to the sellers sincere pleasure that such action was taken prior to placing the property on the market and that the agent made a mistake. With the appraisal in hand, indicating the higher value of the property, the agent can show the property confidently at the higher price. Should the question of price come up during a showing, the agent has an appraisal to substantiate the position.

Objection 11:   *Another agent said that he could get more than you have indicated you can.*

This objection is often a test to determine the seriousness of the agent as to the accuracy of the price being suggested. In other instances it is a truthful disclosure of a representation by another agent. In either case the agent is placed on the defensive.

Regardless of the motivation of the seller voicing this objection, the agent must take a position that is both professional and sensitive. This kind of conflict often has an influential effect on people since it appeals to a very sensitive area: their wallet. The best approach is to study the comparables with the seller again. The agent should show the seller in no uncertain terms that, based on what is happening in the marketplace, it is doubtful that a greater price can be obtained for the property than originally suggested. If the seller insists that the other agent believed that he or she could sell it for more, the agent might ask how the person arrived at the price. Usually, the agent has made no formal presentation to the seller, has not substantiated the findings with facts, and has only tried to convince the seller that he or she believes it can be done. While strong conviction in any selling situation is important, it will never prevail over logic. If sellers cannot understand how the salespeople can do what they say they will, they will not list.

Objection 12:   *We want to try it ourselves for a couple of weeks.*

This objection is telling the agent that the sellers do not feel a need for a REALTOR®. If the agent had succeeded in showing the sellers why, in spite of the fee, they could accomplish more through the REALTOR®, this objection would not have surfaced. Therefore, the agent must home in on the exact objections to using an agent, because something has been unanswered.

The only alternative to probing deeper into the exact reasons for postponing the decision to list is to attempt a firm commitment from the sellers regarding the two-week timetable. If the sellers agree to list with the agent after two weeks, the agent should post-date the listing and have the sellers approve it. This will give them the two weeks necessary in order to try to sell their home themselves, with a professional sales effort ready to go into effect upon the termination of this trial period.

Objection 13:   *Your company is too small (or new).*

In this position, again agents often feel as though they are on the defensive, when they shouldn't. Big is not always best, and numerous new companies have top-quality service. The fact that the firm is new or small puts added demands on the agent to sell the property. Older or larger companies do not need to be as intense about selling.

Objection 14:   *We don't want a lot of people in and out of our house all the time.*

The agent has two logical replies.

    a) Neither do we, Mr. Seller. Our interest is in locating

the right buyer for your home based on information that we obtain prior to showing them any properties, such as the buyers' needs and financial ability to buy. In approaching buyers in this fashion, we are in the best position to eliminate the disinterested or unqualified buyers and thereby ensure your home being shown only to buyers who want and can afford this kind of home.

b) We are in the best position to prevent this. Unfortunately, when a buyer calls you directly, you generally have no way of knowing whether the buyer is able to buy your home. Due to our prequalification interview, we will know the financial position of every buyer whom we bring to your home, which achieves your objective of eliminating an unreasonable amount of showings.

Objection 15:   *I'll give you an open listing but that's all.*

Your reply to this objection should be:

I am afraid that if we were to market your home on an open basis, Mr. Seller, we'd be doing you a grave injustice. Our entire marketing program centers around our taking all the necessary steps in order to locate the proper buyer for your property. Unfortunately, we cannot afford to do this on properties not listed exclusively with our firm. If we did this for you, it would be unfair to the sellers who have listed their homes on an exclusive basis. Most important, it probably would not result in the sale of your home and that is what is most important, isn't it!

Objection 16:   *My attorney will help me with everything.*

This objection is best handled as follows:

It certainly is comforting to know that you have access to an attorney should the need arise, but an attorney's role centers around the legalities of a transaction and that comes after one has a buyer. The REALTOR®'s role is to bring buyer and seller together; without that, there is no need for an attorney. We handle the marketing of your property to the public; it is this exposure and professional marketing effort that brings about a sale.

Exercise:

Using the five-step process, overcome each of the following objections:

1. "We have a friend in the business."
2. "We will list, but only for 30 days."
3. "Your commission is too high."

8

Getting the
Listing Agreement Signed

By and large, people have a difficult time in making decisions. Yet, before any sales can occur, the customer must do just that: make a decision. Therefore, the salesperson must be prepared to initiate conversation that, based on the salesperson's perception of the customer, will put the customer in the position of making a decision: positive or negative, but a decision.

THE CLOSING QUESTION

"The closing question is any question which a salesperson asks, the answer to which confirms the fact that the buyer has bought" (J. Douglas Edwards). This has been widely accepted as the true definition of a closing question. Closing questions should never be designed to manipulate or trick anyone into anything. They are merely designed to cause the customer to make a decision.

One wants to attempt to present the facts truthfully and in such a way as to bring about a positive reaction to the closing question. A negative reaction is still better than no reaction at all. A negative reaction can be identified, and the salesperson can evaluate the changes needed to satisfy the seller. When no decision is made, the salesperson is usually at a loss as to what direction to go.

WHEN TO ASK THE CLOSING QUESTION

The exact time to ask a closing question is difficult to determine. Usually a salesperson goes through a series of sales situations in which he or she asks closing questions at all the wrong times and then develops a sixth sense telling him or her when to close. This leaves the new salesperson at a huge disadvantage since the only thing he or she can do is go out and make some mistakes.

While there is no way to avoid making mistakes, with a little thought one can minimize those inevitable occurrences. The salesperson can be led to the close by discussions with the seller causing the salesperson to feel that the seller is ready to make a decision. In this situation, the salesperson may find himself or herself closing at an early stage of the sales encounter.

Let's use the example of a salesperson who has gone on a listing appointment to talk to a FSBO. While previewing the property, the conversation goes something like this:

SELLER: *How long do you think it will take you to sell this house?*

AGENT: *Based on the average length of marketing time in this area, probably 110 days. Did you think longer?*

SELLER: *No, that would be long enough. How long would we have to vacate the property? If we move before it's sold, could we handle everything without having to come back to town?*

At this point the agent should recognize that the seller is leaning in the direction of doing something quickly, particularly since the conversation indicates an urgency. The smart agent would move directly into a preclosing dialogue establishing an understanding with the sellers as to their agreeability.

AGENT: *We can work out a timetable agreeable to all parties. If you have already moved to your new home in another city, I am sure, barring any unforeseen circumstances, that we can transact everything by mail. Are you being transferred?*

SELLER: *Yes, my company is moving me to Houston and would like me there in 60 days.*

AGENT: *Mr. Seller, since time is of the essence, may I suggest that after looking at the balance of your house we take a moment and I'll explain how we'll approach the sale of your home?*

SELLER: *That would be fine.*

In the preceding dialogue we have responded to the urgent message of the seller and offered the preclosing suggestion of "after looking at the balance of your home may we take a moment and I'll explain how we'll approach the sale of your home?" In this we are recognizing the need to move quickly but not at the expense of the seller. In other words, we are not going to damage our credibility with the seller by stopping the preview of the home and, without having seen the property in its entirety, ask him, "Do you want to list with our company?" Not only would this be a pressure close, but it would be asked of someone not in a position to answer the question intelligently. The obvious response would be along the lines of "well, tell me about your company." Feelings of anxiety would result from things moving too quickly. That would jeopardize the agent's obtaining the listing at all.

The best approach is awareness of how well-informed the seller is and whether he or she is in a position to answer such a question. In the preceding case, the seller was obviously anxious, but not necessarily ready to make the decision to list. Therefore, asking to continue the preview of the property and then showing the seller how to approach the sale kept the agent's approach low-keyed.

One should not mistake this approach of deciding whether the seller is informed enough to make the decision to list for a weakness, thus delaying the listing. If the seller had said that he or she did not have the time to spend with the agent and wanted to list the house, the course of action would have been for the agent to list the house at that time and advise the seller of the details as they proceeded through the evening.

This was not the case. All we had was an anxious seller, one truly not ready to sign the listing agreement. Taking the course of action recommended is most advisable in order to cover all bases and doesn't take that much longer.

The main point is that the agent must *think*. The agent must always ask whether he or she could make a decision knowing as little as the sellers know. If the agent feels that he or she could, then he or she should proceed to ask for the sellers' approval of the listing. If not, the agent should disclose all that the sellers must consider and then, after doing so, ask for the sellers' approval. The agent must always consider the sellers' position and their unfamiliarity with the mechanics of this business.

There are always exceptions. One might deal with a seller who could have been closed after "hello." Rather than go into a seller's home like a bull in a china shop, one must approach the situation carefully, with logic and understanding as a guide and not a wild hope that this is the one-in-a-million who will say *yes* with no effort by the agent.

WHERE TO CLOSE

One closes wherever the agent is when the sellers seem ready to make a decision, no matter where. If they are ready, the agent should ask for their approval.

SAMPLE CLOSES AND HOW TO USE THEM

The best closing techniques appeal to the logical side of the customer and are presented when the seller is in the best position to make a decision. In an effort to give some structural guide to closing questions, I offer the following.

Yes or Yes Close

This close always gives the customer a choice between two things, either of which is a *yes* answer. For instance, the agent asks, "Mr. Seller, would you like us to start running the ad on your home in the *Post* or the *Chronicle*?" This question gives the seller a choice between two newspapers in which the ad on the house could appear. Asking the seller, "Would you like me to start advertising your house?" would give the seller a choice between *yes* and *no*. Of course, the seller can always say *no* to the first example, but this type of close downplays the negative.

Positive/Negative Close

This close allows the seller to weigh the positives against the negatives before a final decision. This is particularly helpful in dealing with people who want to "think it over". In this technique the agent has the people list all the positives derived from listing with the REALTOR® and also all the negatives. The REALTOR® should, of course, help the sellers through this process, pointing out various aspects of his or her marketing program that are positive services available to the seller. The sellers must list anticipated negatives if they use the REALTOR®. Upon completion of both lists, the two are totaled; the one with the highest total is the customers' course of action. A sample dialogue follows.

AGENT: *Mr. and Mrs. Seller, as I understand it, you are concerned about making the proper decision, is that correct?*

SELLER: *(Positive response)*

AGENT: *Let me make a suggestion that helps a lot of my clients. With someone in your position, if it is the right thing to do, the facts will speak for themselves. Let's take a piece of paper and pencil (the agent takes out a piece of paper and pencil) and divide the page in half (the agent draws a line down the center of the page). On the left side we'll put a plus and on the right side we'll put a minus (the agent writes a plus and a minus on the appropriate sides). In the plus column we'll list all the reasons for making a positive decision and in the minus column we'll list all the reasons for making a negative decision. When we've finished, we'll total up the columns and the decision will be made. (The agent hands the pencil and paper to the seller.) Why don't we try it?*

At this point the agent's role becomes one of a counselor. He or she must assist the seller in determining as many positives as possible but allow the seller to determine the negatives.

Comparison Close

In many cases, listings can be closed if only the seller considers the attainment of his or her objectives and weighs them against whatever is seen as negative. This is important because often people have a tendency to allow small negatives to manifest themselves into major problems that don't actually exist. The comparison close allows the agent the opportunity to help the sellers make the comparison between factors in their proper perspective. Following are two examples of how to word the comparison close.

I know that you want   (positive) , so isn't it true that   (negative)   is less important than   (restate positive) ?

While   (negative)   seems vital at this moment, in the long run your ability to   (positive)   dominates your decision, doesn't it?

These are most applicable in instances where the customer has identified a major goal and a minor objection. For instance, by a given date the seller wants the whole family moved to the city to which he or she has been transferred whether the house is sold or not (preferably the former). The objection, however, is centered around the length of the listing. Because of this objective for the move, if the house is not sold, someone will have to be responsible for it after the sellers have moved. The agent's listing agreement for a longer listing period than the seller wants is really a negative that has grown out of proportion because someone might have to handle the property after the move. Since the company would already be involved, this would be a benefit and not a drawback. In this case, one of the following responses would be appropriate.

> *I know that you want to have your family with you as soon as possible, so isn't it true that the length of the listing agreement is really less important than being reunited with your family?*

> *While the length of the listing agreement seems vital at the moment, in the long run your ability to have your family with you in Atlanta really dominates your decision, doesn't it?*

Similar Situation

One of the oldest types of closes is the one that makes the customer aware of what happened to someone else in the same position. Unfortunately, too often this tactic is used as a pressure move to make the customer buy immediately. Anything designed to manipulate is not only unprofessional but offensive and should be avoided. However, if there is such a situation that the agent can relate to the customer, it is incumbent upon the agent to do so as tactfully as possible.

This technique, if used improperly, can devastate the relationship between agent and customer. Conversely, if used properly, this technique can bring about positive responses and help the customer consider all the possible results from their actions.

Example

A seller has a short time to sell her home before she moves to another city. She wants to try to sell the house herself up until the time of the transfer and then, if unsuccessful, turn it over to a REAL-TOR®. This is unwise, since most vacant houses sell for considerably less than the amount paid for occupied houses. An occupied house, being furnished, presents a more homelike environment than the sterile environment of a vacant house. The seller should be aware of this. One might choose to advise the seller that while this decision is, of course, hers to make, she should remember that furnished houses generally sell for more than vacant houses. Perhaps the agent should relate a true story about someone, proving the statement.

> *Ms. Jones, I want you to know that I am eager to help you in any way that I can and, of course, respect that this is a decision that you must make. I would, however, like to advise you of possible situations that would best support your listing your house now as opposed to waiting until you move.*
>
> *In December 1980, Mr. and Mrs. John Doe, who now live in Houston, were in much the same position as you. They chose to list their home before they moved and experienced a sale before they left, at a price netting them what they wanted. We were convinced that the sale occurred at that figure because the property was shown in the best fashion: furnished. I know that your main concern is a quick sale for the most money, isn't it?*

In this example, a situation was used with a positive outcome. It could have been stated to indicate that a previous customer had experienced a prolonged marketing time, which in the long run proved more costly due to the holding cost experienced by the seller in maintaining the payments and upkeep of the home after moving and incurring another house payment. The situation could also have been presented where the former customer received much less than originally anticipated as a result of the vacant home.

In each of these situations, the agent must remember certain important factors. The similar situation must be true. If the agent hasn't experienced such a situation, he or she must find someone in the office who has and use that situation, acknowledging that "this occurred recently to the customer of a fellow agent." When using this technique, one must be prepared to furnish the seller with the name and phone number of the former client so that the seller can, if desired, confirm the situation. Truth in business dealings is essential. When one is prepared to allow the seller to verify what he or she is representing, this immediately enhances the agent in the eyes of the seller.

Cushion

A spinoff from the *similar situation close* is the *cushion*. As in the case of the similar situation close, the cushion arms the agent with a means of drawing a parallel between the customer's situation and other customers with whom the agent has worked and does so in a neat structure.

Basically, the cushion utilizes three primary words: *feel, felt,* and *found.* Using these three key words, the agent extends a degree of empathy as well as support to his or her position with the example of another.

The structure is, "I know how you *feel.* I have had clients who *felt* much the same way that you do, but they *found . . . ."*

Example

In the earlier situation where the seller is being transferred and wants to offer her house as a FSBO as long as she lives in the house, one might say the following.

> *Ms. Seller, I know how you feel about listing your home. I have had customers who felt much the same way as you do, but they found that marketing their house with a REALTOR® prior to their vacating the property allowed the buyers to view the house in its best light, resulting in a quicker sale and at a higher price. That is what's most important, isn't it?*

In this technique, as in the earlier one, the agent must be prepared to share the names and phone numbers of those to whom he or she is alluding.

Order-Blank Close

In many listing situations there is great rapport between the seller and the agent. The seller is receptive to what the agent has presented, and there are no apparent reasons for the seller not to sign the listing. However, the atmosphere is such that no action on the part of the seller results in a signed listing. In this or comparable situations, the *order-blank close* is most effective.

Often the seller is feeling great stress as a result of realizing the need to make a decision, but built-in sales resistance holds him or her back. At this time the agent must take the proper steps to cause the seller to do what he or she wants but otherwise might not. At this moment the agent must initiate this most powerful and most innocent closing technique. The technique is more action than words, because the agent simply begins completing the listing agreement, involving the seller step by step, but definitely filling it in. It is amazing at times how relieved many sellers are that they have made the decision to list; getting the name on the dotted line becomes relatively easy.

This technique should never be used when the agent feels that the seller has unanswered questions. It is only used when in the judgment of the agent the seller has all the necessary information in order to make a decision and when he or she feels that such a decision is warranted.

Example

After a complete and thorough listing presentation by the agent to the seller, the agent unsuccessfully attempts many times to get the seller's approval of marketing the home. Following a serious discussion about what the seller wants to achieve from the sale of the property and sensing the seller's desire to do something definitive, the agent takes the listing agreement out of his briefcase and begins to fill out the agreement, all the while asking the seller questions necessary in order to complete the agreement.

AGENT: *Mr. Seller, what is the exact spelling of your last name?*

SELLER: *Wordsworth, W-o-r-d-s-w-o-r-t-h.*

AGENT: *And what is the legal description of the property? It will be on your copy of the deed or perhaps your copy of the note.*

SELLER: *Excuse me a moment and I'll get that information.*

In this dialogue, we have a most agreeable seller. This technique usually produces such results because it is utilized when the agent senses a great desire on the part of the seller to take definitive steps. However, some responses question the actions of the agent, such as "What are you doing?" or "Why do you want that information?" In this situation the agent must always disclose immediately the reason for the inquiry. "I am interested in the data so that I might complete the necessary information in order to market your property." This is not only true but entirely necessary. The agent has not asked the seller to sign a listing, and the seller should have the requested information on hand.

This technique is extremely effective because until the seller stops the agent, the agent is getting closer and closer to listing. Some people view this technique as high pressure; certainly when used in the wrong situation, it could be. However, the importance of having a variety of techniques is based on the fact that not all will work in all situations. If they did, the agent would need only one technique. Being able to read the situation properly is a critical part of successful selling.

WHAT TO REMEMBER ABOUT CLOSING

The closing is only one part of the sales cycle. It is by no means all that is important nor can it be expected to be effective if not approached with sensitivity and good judgment. As one's career progresses, the agent will develop individual methods of dealing with closing situations. The closing techniques mentioned in this chapter are only guides to use as each agent begins to discover the most effective methods of dealing with different people in selling situations. There is not *one way* to close any more than there is one way to walk. How one does it is not nearly as important as whether it takes the agent where he or she wants to go.

One must always put oneself in a self-analytical frame of mind in an effort to evaluate the effectiveness and direction of what has been done. Only by doing so can one truly develop a particular style of selling. Only after identifying one's style can one apply it with great confidence.

AFTER THE LISTING IS SIGNED

Upon completing the listing interview, the agent should thank the sellers again, let them know that he or she will be in touch within the week (Chapter 9 expands upon this step), and make arrangements for obtaining a key to the property. Before leaving the house, there is another valuable function to be performed: the agent should give the sellers a list of items that will assist in the sale of the property, such as the "Tips to Get Top Dollar for Your Home" which follow. This will get the seller involved and help the agents who show the house.

TIPS TO GET TOP DOLLAR FOR YOUR HOME

1. Yard should be well kept.
2. Driveway should be kept neat and free of clutter.
3. House should be neat for all showings.
4. Pets should be penned.
5. House should always smell pleasant for each showing.
6. Carpets and floors should be kept clean.
7. Air conditioning should be kept in good working order.
8. The home should be available at all times.
9. Owner should not be present when home is shown.
10. Furniture should be clean and in good condition.
11. Stereo music should be playing.
12. All lights should be lit (closets, ovens, garage, etc.),
13. Closets should be neat.
14. The house must be presented in its most desirable condition.

Finally, upon leaving the house with the signed listing, the agent should put up the for-sale sign. While some signs require help to set in place, in most cases signs can be put up by the agent at the time of the listing. The sooner it goes up, the better.

Exercise

Use each of the following closes in three different ways to close a listing situation:

1. Yes/yes close
2. Positive/negative close
3. Comparison close
4. Similar situation close
5. Cushion
6. Order blank close

9

Servicing the Listing and Referral Prospecting

When a property is listed with an agent, it is done with the understanding that the seller of the property is relying on the efforts, judgment, and accountability of the agent. It is essential that the agent understand this and act accordingly.

The quickest way to alienate sellers is by failing to be sensitive to their needs. Every seller needs to be kept informed. To most peo-, ple, a home is the biggest investment that they have ever made; to many the equity in a home represents all the money that they have. Thus, the agent should be prepared to respond to the sellers' unexpressed desire to be kept apprised of the progress of marketing the property. This means to advise regarding all that is, has, and will be done and the effects. Too often the agent takes the position that the sellers aren't going to care about anything but a sale. While this is their primary concern, failing to fulfill obvious obligations only creates a barrier that becomes almost impossible to overcome.

Failing to act in the best interests of the seller often means failing to do whatever the seller feels is in his or her best interest. One can never go wrong if the agent maintains maximum communication with the seller.

COMMUNICATION WITH THE SELLER

While no timetable for contacts with the seller is applicable to all people, a good rule to follow is making contact with all sellers no less than once per week to advise them as to what has transpired on the properties in the past week. Some situations will necessitate

115

accelerating this program to more frequent contacts; under no circumstances should it fall to less than once per week.

A good program is to mark the calendar on Monday of each week as the day to call sellers and report to them. Sometimes, things may prohibit one doing so each Monday. When this occurs, one should call on Tuesday and not put if off for days. If after two days of attempting to contact a seller, one has been unable to do so, other action must be taken. Sending the seller a letter, mentioning the difficulty in contacting him or her, lets the seller know that the effort is being made; the letter should mention that the agent is continuing efforts to make contact. The agent may have a situation in which a seller is out of town. If possible, one should find out where the seller will be and how he or she can be contacted. Each week the agent should call him or her long-distance and advise of progress. This costs a few dollars but does wonders for rapport. If a seller is going to be out of the country or unable to be reached, one must find the address and write about progress, as well as advising a local contact with whom the agent can maintain contact.

Unless one takes steps to maintain a high degree of rapport, the agent runs the risk of having it affected by the seller's interpretation of the efforts or the lack of them. Primarily, the message to communicate to the sellers is a report on exactly what has transpired since the last conversation—how many showings have been made on the property, agents' and customers' comments, suggestions for the sellers regarding the appearance of their property, and plans for open houses, ads, etc.

It is strongly advisable to visit the sellers every 30 days, in addition to the phone contact each week. This does wonders for rapport both in terms of its creation and maintenance. The interesting aspect of rapport is that regardless of how sincere and hard-working one might be, if the house isn't sold or being shown as the seller thinks it should, rapport can break down with anyone. One must work at it.

If there is no news to give the seller, that is no reason not to call. One should call the seller and report that nothing has happened since the last conversation but that better news is anticipated in the coming week. This is better than not calling at all and leaving the seller to deduce what they may, which is rarely kind.

GETTING BUSINESS FROM THE SELLER

Just as with people-to-people PR, all sellers are sources of business contacts and, if worked properly, can prove most fruitful. When houses are placed on the market for sale, people talk; frequently they know others interested in selling. It would be nice if sellers would always call their agent when they had such knowledge; unfortunately they don't. One must ask for it.

When to Obtain Leads from Sellers

The three occasions when listing agents should solicit business from their sellers are (1) when the house is listed, (2) when the house sells, and (3) when the house closes.

When the House Is Listed

When the seller lists his or her home with an agent, he or she is expressing confidence and acceptance of the agent. As this confidence grows, it is wise to inquire of the seller who else is or might be interested in selling. The worst they can say is no one. Example:

> Mr. and Ms. Seller, I appreciate very much the confidence that you have expressed in me and my company by allowing me the opportunity to market your home. My entire income is dependent on my ability to work with people such as yourselves who need a competent REALTOR®. I was wondering if perhaps among the people with whom you socialize, work, or attend church, you could give me the name of a family that I might contact regarding the sale of their home?

When the Home Sells

With the sale of the sellers' property, they are pleased with the agent's services and are more receptive to giving the names of others who might need a REALTOR®. The agent has planted the seed during the appointment resulting in the listing and will generally experience a positive response. Example:

> Congratulations, Mr. and Ms. Jones. I will be in touch with you in the next few days regarding the exact time of the closing. Before I leave, I would like to inquire if perhaps anyone has come to mind who might need my services.

When the Sale Closes

After closing the sale of the property, the sellers have signed all the necessary papers and are aware of the net dollars they are receiving and are generally very pleased. At this time, one should inquire about referrals. Example:

> Mr. and Ms. Jones, may I express how much I appreciate and enjoyed working with you. As always, I am eager to contact others who need the services of a professional REALTOR®. Is there anyone whom you would suggest?

Much time will pass between these occasions. One should not feel that it is too much asking. If the agent doesn't ask, he or she has no one to blame for not receiving.

Following this program, an agent will ask sellers for referrals on three separate occasions. The odds are that during one of these meetings they will have a name or names for the agent. To expect them to give the names voluntarily is wishful thinking.

ADJUSTMENTS IN PRICE AND MARKETING POSITION

Try as one may to predict the marketplace, there are times when the price of a property turns out to be too high and the seller must be approached about reducing the price. This is never an easy task. The problem is not that it becomes necessary but rather how to deal with the problem best.

It is in no way a reflection on the agent when price reductions become necessary particularly during an unstable economic period. Of course, if this happens all the time, perhaps the agent needs to be better prepared when accepting the listing. However, in normal cases, it shouldn't be cause for alarm.

When approaching a seller for a price reduction, one must be able to justify the position. Most of the time sellers are unreceptive to price adjustments; they anticipate a certain amount of money from the sale of the property, and reducing the offered price decreases that amount. Anticipating this is helpful.

Just as when taking the listing, one must prepare an updated market analysis for the sellers and present it along with the old market analysis. The reason for showing both of the market analyses is to remind them of how the market was at the time of the listing (which caused the agent to feel confident about the original listing figure). Then in showing the sellers how the market is now (the change), they are able to appreciate the need for a price adjustment. Different market, different price—it's that simple.

Without the use of a market analysis, this becomes an almost impossible task. The sellers can't understand why they should believe the agent's opinion now when it isn't based on anything more than the first time they followed his or her advice. With a market analysis, however, one has evidence to support not only the recommendation but also the reasoning behind the decision at the time of the listing.

Another aspect frequently in play is the need for more time on the listing. Suddenly the agent discovers that the term of the listing is not enough and must go to the seller and ask for an extension. Many times this can be avoided if the agent is careful and allows enough time when taking the listing, aware of the average marketing period of the other sales in the area. Even then, one may find a need for more time. As with price reduction, the fact that it has occurred is not nearly as crucial as how it is handled.

The best approach is one that begins early. Often agents will wait until the listing is about to expire before they approach the seller about extending the term of the listing. Obviously, this is operating from a weak position since the agent has almost lost control. An important aspect of selling is anticipating problems.

When halfway through the listing, if the listing hasn't sold, one should be preparing the sellers for the possibility of an extension in time on the listing. This is first merely a comment. There are all kinds of reasons for the sellers to grant an extension on a listing. If the sellers decide to use a different REALTOR®, they will basically start all over with someone else. The current agent has the most incentive to sell the property due to the fact that his or her company has invested a great deal of money, time, and effort to market the property; this can only be recaptured if the property is sold. In addition, the machinery is in place; assuming one has maintained a good rapport with the sellers and has been very responsive to their requests, obtaining an extension is not going to be difficult.

One must give considerable thought as to exactly how much additional time one needs. One should not ask for an additional 15 days because one is afraid to ask for the 30 days needed. The agent must decide what is needed and go for it. Returning a second time for another extension will be much harder, so one must get what is needed in the first visit.

The agent must not be afraid to tell the seller that he or she has made a mistake if nothing substantiates the need for more time.

Honesty is always best; we are all human and make mistakes. Making a mistake does not mean that one is a poor agent. Any agent who says that he or she has never made mistakes has not done much business. The mistake is not the problem; repetition of the mistake causes the real problem.

AFTER-SALE FOLLOW-UP

Customers who deal with the agent represent far more business than they have just given. Their future buying and selling and their contacts are many times greater than the business conducted today. For this reason, the agent must take proper steps to solidify the relationship. To do this, one must do what is *not* expected. When a seller hires a REALTOR® to sell a property, the good job that the agent does is not what makes an impression. He or she did not hire an agent anticipating a bad job. The seller anticipated that the agent would do a good job; he or she did and was rewarded handsomely. In no way does this mean that one is entitled to anything more (i.e., referrals, future business, etc.).

However, when the agent goes beyond what is expected and gives that extra something, this deserves a continuing relationship. Some people will not appreciate what the agent has done for them beyond his or her responsibilities, but one day they will. They may be talking with another agent and not feel the same dedication; or discussing with friends a problem that the friends are having with their agent that they didn't experience; or perhaps noticing the positive responses from their friends when conversation takes them into discussing some aspect of the sale of their property and they comment on their agent's role.

Things like thank-you notes and greeting cards throughout the year go a long way. Taking a gift and spending a few moments to visit also help secure the relationship. Taking some of the dollars earned from the transaction and spending them on the seller to express appreciation is not only good judgment but fair and proper. Anything that indirectly says to the customer, "You have worked with an agent who is a cut above the rest, both professionally and personally," cannot be anything but an asset.

Exercise

Explain *servicing* and *referral prospecting*.
When and how do you handle adjustments in price and marketing position?

10

Where Buyers Come From

As with sources of listings, one is led to the same conclusion regarding buyers: they are everywhere. Some sources are more fruitful than others, but basically there is no unproductive source of buyers. The agent must decide what his or her objectives are, in terms of the clientele with whom one wishes to specialize, and pursue them. They are there for the asking.

In arriving at the different sources available, the reader should refer to Chapter 2 and utilize the same process of brainstorming for determining sources of buyers. Some of the most obvious sources are:

- Sellers. They have to move somewhere.
- Property calls.
- People affiliated with moving companies. They know when people are moving into town.
- Travel agents. These people are frequently told the nature of a trip and can be an excellent source of buyers, as many are affiliated with a nationwide network of travel agents. With a little groundwork they could be advised when someone from another city is arranging a trip for a transferee.
- People holding garage sales. When people are planning to move, they usually try to eliminate unneeded items.

- Mortgage companies and savings and loans. Most lenders require advance notice of any impending sale or will assess a penalty for early payoff in excess of the usual payment. Therefore, most sellers notify their lenders. The people who work in these departments are great sources of business.
- Friends and relatives.
- Centers of influence.
- Former customers.
- Chambers of commerce.

The list is literally endless. Yet for some reason most agents will only work a small portion of the sources available to them. The secret to success in selling is maximizing the alternatives available. When working only one or two sources of buyers, ultimately those sources exhaust themselves. The lag time between the time when they prove no longer productive and finally cultivating a new source can be devastating. Justifiably, it is necessary to keep as many irons in the fire as possible.

OBTAINING BUYERS

After the agent has determined which area of the market he or she wishes to pursue and commit himself or herself, one must maintain an active role within that sphere in an effort to obtain buyers. For instance, if one has decided to enroll one's child in little league baseball and to be involved in coaching this team, might it not be a consideration to select a team (if the child has no preference) that will put the individual in touch with children of families most likely to be part of the clientele that one seeks?

If, for example, one wants to deal with the more affluent white-collar workers in one's community, involvement in activities such as social functions, membership in country clubs, active roles within organizations attracting this type of clientele, are essential. This is not to say that one who does not belong to all the "right" clubs and attend all the "right" social gatherings will be unsuccessful in working with these people as buyers. However, one who is active in these areas will have more exposure to this group than one who is not.

One must consider that the socioeconomic makeup of the individuals with whom one comes in contact dictates greatly the most frequent clientele with whom one will deal. This is not to indicate that there is a right or wrong group or area with which to be associated. It is only to acknowledge that the selection of certain activities for the specific purpose of generating business is a wise decision. If one chooses to engage in such pursuits because they are the source of great personal pleasure, the business that one will derive from the activities makes the involvement that much more rewarding.

An example of business-motivated involvement is joining a service organization. It has long been recognized that involvement within such groups can prove rewarding not only personally but also financially. Therefore, if one is going to join a service organization that meets on the east side of town, one must consider whether the individuals within this group will be advantageous for one's business (if another available choice would prove more beneficial). This is in no way being self-centered or unfairly calculating. It is merely honest as to the complete reason for one's involvement and the benefits, and then making the choice that will prove most beneficial. Membership in either group will prove to be a good experience for both the agent and the group; why not choose the group that can best serve one's long-range purposes?

In practically every city across the country one sees this occurring time and time again. The jeweler who owns the exclusive jewelry store catering to the wealthy usually belongs to the organizations and clubs that will make himself or herself highly visible to these potential customers. Why shouldn't REALTOR®s do the same?

We established with door-to-door public relations that in addition to meeting the people within an area we must become a part of the area. This means being active and capitalizing on the exposure that one can enjoy through various activities. This philosophy and approach should be considered when engaging in any area of one's life that could prove beneficial to one's business. To ignore it is foolish and only allows a competitor to gain an advantage for the business that the agent is pursuing and serves to minimize one's alternatives.

All such activities, combined with the prospecting efforts of the agent, result in maximum exposure to the available buyers in the marketplace. One must always be open to additional methods of obtaining new buyers and implementing new methods. Learning from one's successes, failures, and fellow agents is a characteristic of the truly complete real estate professional.

MANAGING BUYERS

Every agent must have a means of organizing the buyers with whom he or she works. As buyers are added to the list of prospective purchasers, they must be prioritized. This must take into consideration:

1. The length of time that the agent has been working with them

2. The length of time they have been looking for a house (buyers who have been in the house market for quite a while tend to take more time than those new to the market)

3. The availability of housing that accommodates the buyers' requirements

4. Financing available in that price range

5. Value of the transaction (not just in terms of commission, but the future business that might be enjoyed as a result of finding the right home for a particular buyer [i.e., wealthy, influential contact; good corporate contact; etc.])

6. Feeling of personal commitment to one buyer over another

This must be weighed in deciding the order to follow in working with buyers. Naturally, plans must be flexible, as the buyer's timetables will not always coincide with the agent's.

One important prerequisite of success is the ability to recognize one's limitations. One cannot be all things to all people; one must be able to accept this in everything one does. This is particularly true in recognizing that one can effectively work with only a certain number of buyers at one time. The agent must be prepared to refer the number of buyers in excess of that maximum to other agents. It is better to receive a referral fee than to lose the buyer completely because one wanted to work with all buyers.

This limit varies with every agent. One thing is certain; for an agent to deal effectively with a great number of buyers (or sellers, for that matter) he or she must have assistance. There must be someone to be delegated some of the work if an agent wishes to achieve his or her potential (this is discussed in Chapter 18). I am hesitant to mention any number of buyers with whom one can actively work, because this is not applicable to everyone. However, the "average" agent would do well to keep up with five active, qualified buyers at any one time.

SERVICING THE INVENTORY OF BUYERS

The agent must consider that there is a certain amount of work associated with every buyer; adequate time must be allotted for each activity. In addition to the time one must spend in qualifying buyers (covered in Chapter 12) and showing houses, one must also locate houses to show, preview the houses prior to showing, visit with the buyer periodically in an effort to maintain a high degree of rapport, and contact each buyer regularly to keep each aware of the agent's activities in trying to find the right home. All these efforts take time. Scheduling one's day around all these activities will not only allow the agent to accomplish more but also allow one to maintain consistency in contacts with buyers. It is the lack of this consistency that ultimately results in a breakdown of rapport and lost sales.

All buyers are interested in dealing with an agent who will help them overcome their problem. What is that problem? It is finding a new home. Therefore, if the agent can maintain a sensitivity to this desire and take a course of action with a buyer that communicates (whether by words or actions) that this is exactly what the agent is doing, fewer buyers will seek other REALTOR®s. In the end the agent will find that he or she will experience greater loyalty from buyers.

Exercise

List five ways to acquire buyers and what type of buyers would come from these suggestions.

Give hypothetical profiles of five buyers obtained from your prospecting sources. Using this profile, prioritize your buyers and ask another student to do so as well. Afterward, compare your order to your fellow student's and see if you differed from one another and why. (Frequently another will see a value that one has overlooked. The more aware one is of various opinions in evaluating buyers, the more one's horizons expand).

11

Effective Telephone Technique

Since the real estate agent spends a great deal of time with telephone calls from potential buyers, it is only fitting that a thorough discussion be made on this subject. The specific area of concern is the technique that one uses in handling incoming calls. Since these calls can be received by a real estate office at any time, most offices have schedules in which the agents can participate, reserving certain times of the day for certain agents to handle calls from prospective buyers and thus putting the agent in touch with individuals representing potential sales. This designated time for the agent to handle the incoming calls is commonly referred to as *property time*, *floor time*, or *opportunity time*. Regardless of what one's office labels this part of the work day, it is a valuable part of the overall sources of income available to the agent.

Though this activity is a significant part of the average agent's work life, the success of most agents while on property time is poor. Surveys show that 70 percent of the buyers who contact a real estate office in their initial stage of looking for a house will contact other offices as well. Of 10 property calls from buyers just entering the market, the average agent will lose 7, and work with only 3. This is not true of every office, but it is an alarming enough statistic to merit an analysis of what happens when on the telephone in an effort to increase the success factor in this area.

WHY IS THE CALLER CALLING?

This question is not as simple as one might think. The immediate response to this question is "to gain information," which is only partially true. The caller is calling for information, but certain forces affecting the caller are usually overlooked and often result in an unsuccessful outcome.

The most reasonable answer to this question is actually "to eliminate the property." Let's investigate what the buyer is experiencing; the validity of this answer will become apparent.

When prospective buyers decide to begin looking for a new home, they will normally look through the ads in the home section of the newspaper for homes which appear to be the type of home in which they are interested. Since the purpose of any real estate ad is to make the buyer call the real estate office offering the property, the ad is usually general and tells buyers only enough to create interest, not enough to allow them to decide whether they should or shouldn't look at the home.

A good example would be found in almost any classified or home section of a newspaper with homes advertised by REALTOR®s. If a family is interested in three-bedroom ranch-style homes in the $80,000 range, there could well be 30 to 130 ads for such homes.

There is more to the selection of a home than the correct number of bedrooms and style of construction. With only this to identify the property, the buyer must call the advertising REALTOR® to obtain additional information. Is it unreasonable to conclude that if a buyer calls in an effort to determine whether a property has the features sought, the buyer is calling to eliminate the property? Let's look further.

If one were to do a bit of research and determine the type of home most in supply in the market, one might be surprised to find the enormous number available. In the preceding example, we used a three-bedroom ranch. If in fact a buyer were looking for such a home and circled perhaps 40 such ads in the newspaper, is it reasonable to expect that this buyer would have even the most remote interest in viewing every home? Does any buyer want to look at 40 homes even if they are all very close to what is desired?

With few exceptions, people do not wish to spend a great deal of time viewing property unless it is worth their time. Most buyers would want to narrow the 40 homes down to 10 or less. Therefore, when a buyer calls on a property, the buyer is calling in an effort to gain information to eliminate the property from his or her selection.

SALESPERSON'S OBJECTIVES

The objectives of the salesperson are to obtain the name, telephone number, and appointment with the caller, with the emphasis on the appointment. Most property calls made by buyers are on houses in which they will actually not be interested. Surveys show that less than 11 percent of the buyers who call on an ad will, upon seeing the property, be interested in the house. Less than 33⅓ percent of the buyers who call on a sign will be interested in the property upon seeing it and learning the price.

Therefore, the agent should be aware that most property calls are from buyers who will need to be shown other homes. This should be of no surprise since the general nature of the ad cannot possibly lead to any other conclusions. This is also true on sign calls. Though the percentages are better on sign calls than on ad calls, the fact that the buyer will live inside the house and not outside makes the showing of the property subject to a great possibility of having to show other homes. Additionally, many buyers call on houses with for-sale signs without any knowledge of the price range of the property. When the price is beyond their means, they must be made privy to information on other homes.

The need to set one's sights on the ultimate objective of obtaining the appointment is essential. In fact, one might conclude that the only reason an agent should ever use the phone is to get an appointment.

THERE ARE NO BAD PROPERTY CALLS

Frequently agents find themselves commenting on the quality of a property call. All too often the property calls that are warm and friendly are considered good ones and the ones that are quick and hostile are bad. Nothing could be further from the truth. When an individual calls a real estate office he or she is expressing a need or desire to buy or sell real estate; it is up to the salesperson to encourage the caller to do so. Therefore, we can conclude that there are rarely if ever bad property calls.

This is a typical example of what causes such a judgment, and the problems that occur as a result.

An agent on property time receives a call from a prospective purchaser.

AGENT: *Good morning, ABC Realty. May I assist you?*

CALLER: *Whom am I speaking with, please?*

AGENT: *This is John Agent.*

CALLER: *John, this is Jim Buyer. I have got a problem and I need your help. I am being transferred here with my company; my wife, my children,*

> *and myself are staying at the Holiday Inn. My*
> *company will handle all the financing of our*
> *new home. Our furniture is on the moving*
> *company's truck and is on its way here now.*
> *My company has given me a $10,000 check to*
> *use as a deposit as soon as we find a home. I*
> *must buy a house today. Can you help me?*

This is, of course, a *good* property call; any agent would welcome such a call. To carry our example further, Jim and his family go with John Agent to look at homes for an entire day. Properties are all wrong; John is unprofessional and of no help; the day was a complete waste of their time. As a result of this bad experience, Jim calls on another ad the next day and decides that he is not going to get involved with an agent. The conversation goes as follows.

AGENT: *Good morning, XYZ Company. May I help*
         you?

JIM: *(very cold) Yes, you have a house advertised in*
         the Elmwood Addition. I'd like to have the ad-
         dress.

AGENT: *I would be happy to show that house to you;*
         would this afternoon be convenient?

JIM: *(angrily and almost shouting) Let me tell you*
         how it is going to be. You're going to give me
         the address of that house. I'm going to drive by,
         and if I like it, I'll call you. If not, I'll call
         another agent. Do you understand?

This would be called a *bad* property call. In reality this is a better property call than when Jim called John Agent the day before. It is better because the urgency to buy is even greater than the day before as a result of the day lost with the unprofessional John Agent. Yet, in most cases the labeling of this as a bad property call results from the agent's negative reaction to the attitude projected by the caller.

If only the agent would remember that there are no bad property calls and that the attitude transmitted by the caller may result from a bad experience and has nothing to do with the true nature of the individual or the relationship that the salesperson will experience with the caller. Maintaining a healthy attitude is crucial. The agent must not allow the attitude of the customer to become an unfair influence over his or her attitude.

PROBLEMS INHERENT IN HANDLING PROPERTY CALLS

The traditional position of the real estate agent during property time is unreasonable. The idea of being expected to remember everything about every property that the company has on the market is not only unfair but nearly impossible.

For decades the sign of an agent's sales ability was skill in keeping the conversation going. When a property call came in on a home, if the agent could avoid stammering and stuttering through the conversation with the caller, this was the sign of a *good* agent. The idea that a salesperson is measured by his or her ability to avoid the nervous barriers that are so crippling to so many is insulting. When a property call comes into a real estate office, the customer must get answers to questions during the conversation with the agent. Otherwise the caller will feel skeptical, regardless of how smooth the agent might be. For example:

AGENT: *Hello, ABC Realty. May I help you?*

CALLER: *Yes, you have a house advertised in the Elmwood Addition. Could you tell me something about it?*

AGENT: *(Flipping through the listing book frantically trying to find a copy of the listing) Yes, this is a beautiful home. I would be delighted to show it to you. Would this afternoon be convenient?*

CALLER: *Well, possibly, but could you tell me something about it?*

AGENT: *(Now desperately looking elsewhere on the desk and in desk drawers for a copy of the listing, with no success) Yes, sir, this is a very comfortable home. If you would like to see it, I'd be happy to show it to you.*

CALLER: *Are you going to tell me something about this house?*

AGENT: *(Completely unable to locate the copy of the listing of the house in question) Well, sir, this house just defies description. You really have to see it to appreciate it. Could I pick you up and show it to you? Hello? Are you there?*

Obviously the caller was well aware that the agent was

experiencing a problem. Unfortunately, the suspected problem transmitted to the caller is actually worse than what occurred (the fact that the agent was unable to locate a copy of the listing). The caller thinks that he or she is talking to an uninformed idiot; hope of salvaging the situation is usually lost.

The illustration of a lost copy of the listing is only one situation that can cause the agent to fail to come across as knowledgeable. Those who have not yet faced this problem will, because it comes to all at one time or another. The only way to avoid such an occurrence is to avoid the situations that cause them by means of careful preparation.

Remembering Everything

Probably the biggest problem in dealing with mistakes during property time arises from the feeling that one should be capable of remembering everything. Most agents will preview new listings that their companies put on the market every week so that they are in a better position to represent the property. This, of course, will prove true to a point, but how long is one's memory of the property accurate? If the home is placed on the market for 180 days and the agent previews the property during the first week, how long is the agent competent to represent the property accurately? If the agent doesn't show the house for the first five months and then during the sixth month of the listing gets a property call on the house, is he or she at a loss? It has been approximately five months since the agent has seen the house. How much can the agent possibly remember? The agent has probably seen hundreds of houses since previewing the house in question. Combine the time lapse with the confusion of all the other houses, and the agent is not much better off than the agent who has not seen the house at all.

If some still reject this as a problem and feel that the agent should be able to remember all the houses on the market, one should consider the limit of one's ability. If a real estate company has 50 or 60 houses on the market, any one of which could be the subject of the property call, is it reasonable to expect the agent to remember everything about each? More specifically, if we were to list by addresses all the houses that a company had on the market, could an agent of that company recite the answers to the following questions about each property:

- What kind of floor is under the carpet in every room?

- How many tons of air conditioning?
- What size is the heating unit?
- What is the age of the roof?
- How far are the schools?

If the firm's inventory numbers only 2 or 3, then perhaps this would not become such an arduous task. If there are 50 homes, this would be next to impossible. The availability of information in a listing book is no salvation, because inquiries must be located and that takes time.

THE IDEAL SITUATION

One must view the world the way it is, think about how one would like it to be, then find a way to bridge the gap. In the area of selling real estate, it would be nice if the customary and accepted way of looking for a house was for the buyer to complete a form that included a financial statement of the buyer, a credit report, verification of savings showing the adequate funds necessary, and a list of the specific houses of interest. This would be mailed to the REALTOR®, and the buyer would wait for the REALTOR®'s call.

This is unrealistic, but let's examine the immediate benefits derived from this type of contact with the REALTOR®. Aside from the fact that the REALTOR® would already have most of the necessary financial information, he or she would know, prior to any conversation with the purchaser, the houses that were of interest. Prior to contacting the purchaser, the agent could review the properties, reacquaint himself or herself with the properties, and locate any other appropriate properties. This is a tremendously confident and secure position for the agent. To some degree, it is one that the agent can create.

SEVEN STEPS TO SUCCESS

This technique is designed to come as close as possible to the ideal in the preceding "fantasy" and works with tremendous success when used properly:

1. Greeting
2. Urgency to return the call
3. Regreeting

4. Statement
5. Question
6. Pivot for an appointment
7. Appointment close

AGENT: *(Greeting) Good morning, ABC Realty. May I help you? (This step is merely a polite and enthusiastic greeting.)*

CALLER: *You have a three-bedroom house advertised in Elmwood. I'd like to know something about it, please.*

At this point the agent should immediately write down the words that the caller uses to identify the property and refer to the property in the same fashion. Most real estate agents tend to refer to property by the street address, while the address of the property is rarely in the ad. Therefore, if the caller inquires about a three-bedroom home in Elmwood, it would be a mistake for the agent to refer to the house as the Voss Road property.

AGENT: *(Urgency to return the call) I don't have that file in front of me at the moment, but if you'll give me your name and number, I'll be happy to call you right back.*

This step is designed to create a logical and acceptable reason to return the call. At this point the caller has obtained none of the desired information; therefore, he or she still needs the agent. Since the caller wants the information that the agent possesses, there is no fear of giving the wrong phone number; this would not serve the caller's best interest.

The important aspect of this step is that it is done quickly and without hesitation. Following this step, the caller will give his or name and telephone number; the agent should repeat the phone number to the caller for confirmation. The agent should thank the caller and repeat that he or she will call right back; the agent then waits for the caller to hang up. This is to avoid the abruptness of the disconnect in the caller's ear and to allow the caller, if necessary, the opportunity to come back to the line with any last-minute requests such as other properties.

At this point, the agent should use the cross-reference directory to determine where the caller lives. If the caller happens to be a neighbor of the sellers, the caller is probably interested in information to help in the sale of his or her home. This is important information for the agent. If however, the caller is not a neighbor, the agent should so note this information on the agent's property call recorder (Figure 11-1).

Salesperson _____   Date _____Time _____

Caller's Name _____
Address _____
Home Phone _____
Work Phone _____

Purpose of Call _____
Source of Call _____
Information _____
          _____
          _____
          _____

Appointment? _____   Date _____

If no appointment, follow-up plans _____
_____

Notes: _____
       _____
       _____
       _____

Figure 11-1. Property Call Record

The next task for the agent is to pull a copy of the listing in question, review the information, and pull information on comparable homes in the area that the agent feels that he or she might wish to bring to the attention of the caller. These should be gathered on all advertised properties prior to property time in order to eliminate the agent's searching for comparable properties while handling property calls. The agent phones the caller and proceeds to the next step.

AGENT: *(Regreeting) Hello, Ms. Caller, this is John Agent, and I have the information on the three-bedroom ranch-style home in Elmwood that you called about.*

This, obviously, is merely identifying oneself to the prospective buyer both by name and property.

AGENT: *(Statement) This is a lovely home nestled among majestic trees on a beautiful and picturesque lot.*

In this step the agent is merely whetting the prospective buyer's appetite, while not being specific about anything. This is in an effort to avoid commenting about what may not be a plus to the caller.

AGENT: *(Question) By the way, Ms. Caller, how many are in your family?*

CALLER: *My husband and I have two children.*

This step causes the caller to speak. A conversation goes two ways; to avoid the agent's being overbearing with the prospective caller, this step is purposely designed to cause the conversation to flow between agent and buyer.

AGENT: *(Pivot for an Appointment) Ms. Caller, based on the size of your family, this home certainly has the correct number of bedrooms, but so do 50 to 60 other homes on the market. Ms. Caller, I would like to have the opportunity to visit with you and your family and determine everything that you are looking for in your new home. Then I can take the task of looking at all those homes off your shoulders and put it on mine. I will narrow down the selection to perhaps 5 or 6 homes in keeping with what you are looking for; you can spend your time looking only at those homes consistent with your needs. I'm sure that you'd prefer to look at 5 or 6 homes very much on the order of what you want, rather than 50 or 60, most of which are not, wouldn't you?*

This step is designed to express the beneficial reasons for the caller to grant an appointment with the agent. It also allows the agent the opportunity to change the discussion from the home in question and focus on the best method to use to locate the proper home for the caller and her family. It is an important and most crucial step.

CALLER: *Well, that certainly would eliminate a lot of wasted time.*

AGENT: *(Appointment Close) Might this evening at 6 be convenient or would 7 be better?*

This step is designed to close the conversation with an appointment. The agent has already established the necessity for doing so; closing at this juncture is only natural.

CALLER: *Seven o'clock would be fine.*

The agent was able to arrive at the appointment rather easily; it will be just this easy for most property calls. However, some callers will refuse the appointment at this point and request more information. When this happens, the agent simply moves back to step 4 (statement).

Example

After the agent goes through step 6, giving the caller a justifiable reason for an appointment, and proceeds to step 7 and attempts to obtain the appointment, the caller responds negatively. The following occurs:

CALLER: *Well, can you tell me something else about the house?*

AGENT: *(Statement) You'll be glad to know that this house is located in walking distance to all the public schools in the area. (Question) Incidentally, Ms. Caller, what are the ages of your children?*

CALLER: *We have a daughter 14 and a son 11.*

AGENT: *(Pivot for an Appointment) I am sure that it would be delightful to know that you will never have to carpool your children to school again, but there is more to a new home than the right number of bedrooms and the distance to schools. Ms. Caller, I truly believe that it would be in the best interest of you and your family if we could take a little time before we begin looking at homes to establish exactly what you want to see in an effort to avoid the endless showings that so many people find*

> *themselves involved in when trying to find a*
> *new home.*

AGENT: *(Appointment Close) Could we get together*
this afternoon or would this evening be better?

CALLER: *Come by at 7:30 tonight.*

Throughout this technique the agent is following an orderly sequence and always approaches the objective of an appointment with prudence and logic from the caller's perspective. The only way that any technique will be effective is if it is logical and in the best interest of the parties involved.

HANDLING TWO DIFFICULT QUESTIONS

All agents find themselves in the dilemma of dealing with various questions from prospective callers when on property time. Various approaches have been recommended for the proper handling of these problems. Many are effective and some leave much to be desired. While following the seven steps to success, the agent must incorporate methods of dealing with specific "disqualifying questions" (questions that could eliminate the property or cause the conversation between agent and caller to terminate). How one does this will have a great bearing on success on the telephone.

Price of Property

In responding to inquiries about the price of a property, the idea of answering all questions with questions is a good technique in maintaining control over the conversation and being assured of receiving information as well as giving it. However, one must be sure that the caller's question is answered prior to responding with a question. If asked for the price of a property, the agent should give the price and then ask for the caller's price range, rather than only asking for the caller's price range.

Example — Incorrect Use of This Technique

CALLER: *What is the price of the property advertised in*
the Elm Grove Addition?

AGENT: *What price home were you looking for?*

This approach is incorrect because it ignores the caller's question. It not only leaves the caller with an unanswered question but also takes a hard-sell position. This occurs due to the agent's attempt to ignore the motivation behind the call (price of property) and then questioning the caller, which could easily be interpreted as manipulative.

Example – Correct Use of This Technique

CALLER: *What is the price of the property that you have advertised in the Elm Grove Addition?*

AGENT: *That property is $95,000. How much had you intended to invest?*

This approach is correct because it answers the question asked by the caller and then follows immediately with a question that maintains the conversation and allows the agent to respond encouragingly, thereby holding the caller's interest. The use of the technique in this fashion allows the agent to ascertain important information and does so in a low-keyed fashion which is in no way manipulative. The only difference between this and the previous incorrect use is the answer that the agent gives the caller.

An important insight is gained from these examples. Manipulation can frequently be identified as a result of the salesperson's failure to acknowledge the questions or opinions of the customer. Obviously, the techniques that advocate ignoring comments or questions that don't support the direction in which the agent wishes the conversation to travel are of a hard-sell nature and can bring about devastating results. One should never ignore anything mentioned or questioned by a customer. To do so is to set oneself up for failure.

Address of Property

"What is the address of the house advertised in the Memorial Area?" This kind of question is a thorn in the side of all real estate agents. It has been debated for a millennium as to the proper way to handle such a request and still reach a desirable end. The only way to respond responsibly to such a query is first to examine everything involved in reaching the proper decision. There are several considerations; one should explore them all.

From the seller's position the only potential benefit from the agent's giving the address of their property to a property call is that possibly someone will look at the house who would not otherwise. The caller's driving by may result in the sale of the property. Unfortunately, the seller is exposed to far more negatives than this single advantage (which itself is questionable since it assumes that there is no way to prevail upon this type of caller to view the house with an agent). The real strength that a home has is the life style that it affords. This can never be determined by a buyer who eliminates property because of the exterior of a home. While, of course, every buyer is attracted to certain styles of homes, the fact remains that one lives inside the house, not outside. If the buyer judges the house based on the exterior appearance, the odds are that he or she will never see the inside of the house. Isn't it a shame to allow such a judgmental situation, when, had the buyer seen the entire home, a sale might have resulted?

Additionally, when an unidentified caller is given the address of a seller's home, how does the agent know to whom he or she is giving the address? While the chance of a problem resulting from disclosing the seller's address is remote, the possibility exists. This is a different situation entirely from someone driving by and seeing the for-sale sign. When a caller has seen a for-sale sign, his or her knowledge of the property is limited to the exterior of the home. When one reads an ad on a property with all the flowery and attractive phrases such as magnificently decorated or luxurious interior (not to mention an indication of price), this can cause speculation about expensive items within the home. One might assume that such a house is owned by someone of means, perhaps with furs or jewels. Should such a conclusion be drawn from the ad, and should a caller with devious intentions call, in giving the address of the property the agent is playing into the caller's hands.

From the agents' position, he or she can be hurt enormously by giving out addresses. Statistics show that advertising produces the poorest results as a source of sales. Since the only purpose of an ad is to make the phone ring, the ad must be general enough to do just that and in no way disqualify itself from consideration by the caller. Once a person drives by the house on which he or she has called, the odds are that he or she will not be interested. In this situation, the customer must look further. However, since the caller supposedly only calls on those houses with attractive exteriors, the agent never has a chance to show the caller other properties.

Giving out addresses is also a potential violation of the fiduciary relationship. Rarely does a listing presentation fail to bring out the fact that the agent can help provide the seller with privacy. This is accomplished by the agent's ability to prevent anyone from seeing the house unless accompanied by a licensed professional agent. When such a comment is made, it becomes part of the oral contractual agreement between seller and agent, just as when the agent tells the seller the freqency with which the REALTOR® will advertise the property. If a promise of advertising is made, in writing or not, it must be fulfilled if the agent is to adhere to the spirit of the fiduciary relationship. The same is true of the promise to assist with privacy. If the agent is to indicate ability to provide a shield from the public, it must occur. Giving an address to a caller is potentially an infraction of the fiduciary relationship, should the caller decide to go to the seller's door and ask to see the house.

If a passer-by, seeing the for-sale sign, asks such permission, the seller should not allow entry but call the agent immediately and make the buyer wait outside until the agent arrives. This potential invasion of privacy cannot be avoided due to the sign, but it is stopped from becoming a problem when the person is denied entry. In the case of the buyer who is given the address, the agent has created the problem; this must be avoided.

From the buyers' position, they actually gain little when receiving the address from the agent. True, they are able to pursue new homes as they desire; from a practical standpoint, that is all that they obtain. They have no individual constantly on the lookout for a home meeting their needs. As vast as most marketplaces are, the involvement of such an individual is a necessary part of finding a new home.

Based on this logical understanding of the benefits and disadvantages experienced by all agents, we must examine how one might best achieve the proper conclusion to the question of giving out addresses. One should begin by establishing this procedure with the seller at the time of the listing so that the seller not only understands but agrees. It should always be a practice to avoid divulging property addresses. The following technique can easily be applied.

After returning the caller's call, as described in the seven steps to success, and being confronted with a request for the address of the advertised property, the agent can respond as follows.

AGENT: *Ms. Jones, I'd be delighted to give you the address of this property, but I am bound by contract with the seller not to give out the address.*

Though this is often enough to get the appointment with the caller, sometimes one may persist and respond with the following.

CALLER: *What are you talking about! Everybody gives out addresses. Do you want me to call another agent and get the address!*

AGENT: *I understand how you feel, Ms. Jones, but if I had your property on the market and you had specifically instructed me not to give out the address, you'd want me to honor your instructions, wouldn't you!*

At this point, the agent must operate from a position of belief, belief in the fact that this course of action is the only course of action to take. The agent must be prepared to follow it no matter what the caller may suggest. A caller trying get the address will make all kinds of promises of business and referrals if the agent will give the address. Such enticements cannot cause the agent to deviate from what the agent knows morally is the proper thing to do.

In over a decade of handling property calls and taking this approach to those who request addresses, I have never known of anyone who called another agent and bought the house. If it did happen once or twice during a 10-year period, that is an insignificant number in comparison to those who chose to get together with me in order to see the house and bought. More importantly, I feel secure about all the actions that I have ever taken on behalf of my sellers. This is the real benefit from such an attitude.

The buyers are in a position of making a decision; either they set an appointment with the agent or contact another agent. Since the agent called is associated with the listing company, he or she is more knowledgeable about the property, and buyers will usually grant the appointment.

Exercise

Utilizing the seven steps to success, structure a dialogue between an agent and a caller to illustrate the proper use of this technique.

12

Qualifying the Buyer

One of the biggest problems experienced by real estate agents is the endless numbers of showings before the buyer finds the "right" one. The problem centers around the fact that the buyer shouldn't be trying to find the "right" home, but rather the agent should be "matching" the buyer to the home. Most of the time agents spend so much time showing houses because they don't know what the buyer wants. Qualifying the buyer effectively enables the agent to locate the home best suited to the buyer.

WHERE TO QUALIFY

Ideally, the agent should qualify the buyer in the buyer's home, whether he or she owns or rents. This is, of course, providing the buyer lives within a reasonable proximity to the agent's office. An easy guide is to determine if the agent would take a listing in the buyer's current neighborhood. If the answer is yes, then the agent should go to the buyer's home to conduct the qualifying interview. If, however, the buyer lives a great distance from the agent's office, the agent should have the buyer come to the office, but the preference is to have the interview in the home of the buyer.

It becomes difficult to ascertain exactly what the purchaser wants in the new home or what the new home must accommodate if one bypasses the inspection of the purchaser's home. The important factor is to see how the buyer lives, the furniture, and the style of living.

ESTABLISHMENT OF RAPPORT

As in all cases of dealing with a customer, the establishment of rapport is essential to a continuous relationship. Starting with the qualifying interview in the home of the buyer, the agent has an opportunity to relax the buyer with the help of familiar surroundings. No matter how comfortable one tries to make an office, it is never as relaxed to the customer as the atmosphere in the home.

The most important areas of rapport center around *like, understand, believe,* and *trust.* The customer must like the agent (not love but at least not find the agent offensive), understand and believe what the agent says, and above all feel that the agent can be trusted. In transmitting this to the potential customer, the agent should approach the situation in a low-keyed but controlled manner. One must allow plenty of time for the interview, avoid being rushed, and be certain to take a few moments to get to know the buyers and their family (where are they from, how long they have lived in the area, the ages of the children, what they do for a living, etc.). These inquiries give valuable information that will allow one to relate to the customer in areas other than business. This approach cultivates rapport.

In the process of cultivating rapport, the agent should ask the customer to allow the agent to see the entire house or apartment. In doing so, the agent can better understand what the customer is used to and has opportunities to identify similar areas of interest.

DETERMINING DOMINANT BUYING MOTIVE (DBM)

One primary objective is to determine the dominant buying motive (DBM). It is usually the one motive with the least amount of flexibility. Buyers can have many motives. They will often compromise many of these, but the dominant buying motive is rarely compromised. Frequently the DBM will only be ascertained following the assimilation of the information discussed during the qualification interview.

Buyers' main reasons for buying a new home generally center around one or more of the following:

- **Pride.** The buyers want the pride and prestige of living in the most exclusive area of town.
- **Profit.** The buyers are looking for their first home, something located in an area that is rapidly appreciat-

ing in value. Their objective is to invest now, sell in a few years, and invest in a nicer home. Appreciation and equity build-up are the main concerns so the motive is profit.

- **Need.** A large family with lots of pets needs to buy a home. Renting is out of the question.
- **Love.** The buyers are very education-oriented and, out of love for their children, want them to attend the finest schools. Therefore, they choose to look for homes in the jurisdiction of the best schools.
- **Fear.** From concern for the welfare of the children, the buyers want to be on a cul-de-sac or little-traveled street so that their children will not be vulnerable to accidents.

DETERMINING NEEDS, WANTS, DESIRES, AND ABILITY TO PAY

There are four basic areas for which every agent should qualify the buyer. They are needs, wants, desires, and ability to pay.

After completing the tour of the buyer's home the agent should suggest to the buyers that they go to an area where they can talk and discuss the buyer's new home. The kitchen table or dining room table is ideal.

Since knowing where to begin is so important, one must guide the conversation in the area of the desired features in the new home rather than the financial aspects of the investment. This must take place early and in great detail. Should the conversation regarding the financial aspects of the purchase be discussed too early, it can cause a barrier. One must know what the buyers want in their new home before knowing where to look.

Needs

This represents the absolutely essential requirements for the new home. Asking the question for this response is not always easy, but the following will accomplish the objective:

Mr. and Ms. Jones, what do you like most about the home (or apartment) you live in now?

This question, though general in its scope, probes into the favorable aspects of the buyers' current residence. After they respond the agent must follow with:

And what do you like the least?

The relationship between these two questions is real. After asking these questions, the agent knows what aspects of the current style of living the buyers enjoy and dislike the most. This is important information but is, of course, often limited to those areas that stand out in the minds of the purchasers. Therefore, to draw more specific bits of information, these questions should be followed by:

Mr. and Ms. Jones, what is there about the kitchen that you are particularly pleased with? the master bedroom? the dining area?

This series of questions asks the same things as in the first question but of a more specific nature. The agent goes room by room and finds out what the buyers like the most about every aspect of the house. This is then followed by:

And is there anything that you dislike about the kitchen? the master bedroom? the dining room?

As before, the agent makes specific inquiries about what the buyer perhaps dislikes.

One should first make the inquiries about the whole house and then room by room in order to judge the priority of the buyers' comments. Those answers to the first series of questions (likes and dislikes about the entire residence) generally center around what is most and least desirable. Though the second group of questions (the likes and dislikes, room by room) is certainly not to be ignored, it is generally not as important as the first group.

What advantage is there to knowing the buyers' likes and dislikes about the current house or apartment? The agent will gain insight as to what the new home must offer.

Wants

This area of the qualification interview addresses the improvements in the buyers' style of living. This can easily be accomplished by asking:

What must you have in your new home?

This allows the buyers to express everything desired in the new home. Though some responses may not seem practical, the agent must not pass judgment. He or she is on a fact-gathering mission to assist in locating the buyers' new home. All comments from the purchaser should be encouraged. If, following this question, the agent feels that there is perhaps more than has been expressed, he or she should add:

> *And is there anything especially important that you want?*

The agent should suggest every room that the buyers failed to include in their list of wants, (i.e., family room, kitchen, children's rooms, etc.)

Additional information regarding wants can be obtained by determining whether the customers have seen anything that they like. Perhaps they have looked at homes prior to the agent's visit and have some specifics in mind. It would do the agent well to find out what they had seen and, rather than the customer describing it, ask for the address of the property and inspect it personally. Having the opportunity to see exactly what the buyer finds acceptable is tremendously beneficial.

Desires

At this point, the agent will have a wealth of information regarding the needs and wants of the buyer. Though this is far more than one usually ascertains about a buyer, the agent can discover more. Everyone would like certain things someday in a new home. The agent should attempt to uncover these. One can do so by simply asking:

> *If you could have any kind of home, regardless of price, what kind of home would you have?*

This allows the buyers to express everything that they have always wanted. Most know that they cannot afford such a home, but this information is valuable to the agent. First, every buyer represents more business than what is being conducted today. Part of that business centers around the next houses in which they will invest. Having advance knowledge of a buyers' ultimate goals gives the agent an edge over others for the customer's future business. Second, sometimes one can locate a home in the price range of the buyer with perhaps one feature that the buyers wanted in the future. If the agent is aware of this, he or she is in a better position to identify to the greatest degree the kind of home in which the buyers will be interested.

Ability to Pay

Once the agent has determined everything that the buyers want in their new home, he or she must determine their financial ability. In dealing with an acquaintance (and therefore certain of financial ability), this point might, at the discretion of the agent, be eliminated. Otherwise, one should begin the discussion by asking:

> *Mr. and Ms. Jones, in order for me to determine the best way for us to go about investing in your new home, there are a few questions that I would like to ask. Would that be all right?"*

This question does nothing more than ask permission to ask a question. The advantage of using this as a lead-in is getting the buyers' positive response, which serves as their permission to ask the necessary financial question, rather than boldly asking how much money they earn.

We have all been taught from an early age not to discuss personal finances with others. Consequently, there is immediate resistance to questions regarding one's financial situation. However, the purchasers must reveal this to someone before securing financing; they may as well start with the agent. One of the biggest problems in dealing with buyers is knowing what price range of houses should be shown. The information gathered by the agent may indicate that the kind of house necessary to satisfy a buyer may cost $125,000, but how is one to know whether the buyer can afford that? It is frustrating to locate the right home for a buyer, have them make the offer to buy, get the offer accepted, and then have them turned down on a loan due to lack of income or personal net worth. Furthermore, such a situation complicates the relationship in pursuing another home.

In times of tight money markets and high interest rates, the best alternative for the buyer is purchasing a home by bypassing a conventional lender and consummating the transaction through some other form of financing (i.e., second mortgages, contract for deeds, and owner financing). There is no way to guide a buyer unless one knows his or her financial position. How would a buyer feel if, after finding the right home, buying it, and getting locked into a long-term high-yield mortgage, he or she later discovered that the agent could have advised the buyer to arrange something at 5 or 6 percent less? A buyer would find little comfort in the fact that the agent followed the buyer's instructions and found the home desired and the buyer took care of the financing. Every buyer is entitled to the best advice possible from an agent. Part of that is the benefit of the agent's knowledge of financing alternatives. Therefore, in order to truly give the most professional service possible, the agent must discover the financial ability of the purchaser in order to know in what direction to guide the buyer.

After asking this question regarding the buyer's permission to ascertain information, the agent should ask both parties (starting with the one who seems the dominant of the two):

Where are you employed?

How long have you been there?

What is your position with the company?

What is your approximate annual income?

These are four simple but important questions. The first three show quality and stability of employment and income, and the fourth, the amount of income. After the buyers answer (and it is amazing how easily they will respond to these questions), the agent should continue with:

Do you have any other sources of income?

How much of your savings have you intended to invest in your new home?

Do you need to sell any property or securities before you invest in your new home?

If additional funds are necessary to invest in the home that is best for you and your family, are such funds available?

In what form?

Do you have any equities in other properties?

Ideally, what kind of monthly investment (payment) would you like to make on your new home?

These questions are designed to reveal the capacity of the buyer in terms of what he or she can afford, if so desired, and would like to spend. In no way should an agent try to extend the purchaser further than the purchaser wishes; by the same token, it is not up to the agent to decide what the buyer feels is affordable. It is the job of the agent to advise the buyer what will be necessary in order to invest in the desired home. Most buyers have not been in the home-buying market for some time; as a result, they often feel that they can invest in the kind of home that they want for far less than it will actually cost. Consequently, if the buyer gives a series of requirements for a new home requiring more money than the buyer had wanted to invest, the buyer must be so advised.

Knowing that the buyers have the financial wherewithal certainly makes life easier. Additionally, if the buyers' requirements indicate a home selling for more than the buyers' capacity, one must determine if they have any way of raising additional monies. Otherwise, this is an exercise in futility.

No one can advise the buyer of his or her alternatives unless one knows the financial capacity of the purchaser. Should resistance be encountered from the purchaser to these questions, the agent must stand firm. The answers to these questions must be obtained if one expects to help the purchaser effectively. Many times when resistance arises, all the purchaser needs is a little reassurance, such as "Everything we are discussing is in the strictest of confidence." (*Note:* Due to varying loan qualification requirements, local lenders should be consulted as to specific ratios of income to loan in an area.)

WILL THEY MAKE THE FINAL DECISION?

One of the most frustrating things when dealing with buyers is to work one's heart out in finding the best home, and have them mention that they want to wait until their parents have seen the house to make a decision. One can do little when such a request is made. In addition to the time required to begin working with additional individuals, the agent is placed in a position that does not make his or her life any easier. The couple had made a decision based on all the houses shown. These new individuals must make a decision based on one house.

This is a difficult position and usually necessitates showing the new people all the other houses in hopes of leading them to the same conclusion. Additionally, the new people feel the need to comment on everything from the most favorable house to the type of offer that the buyer should make. This generally results from the position of responsibility in which they are placed. Had they been involved from the beginning, and the agent had the opportunity to establish rapport and build confidence with them, much of this new problem could have been avoided.

The time to discover the potential of such a situation is during the qualification interview. The last part of this interview concerned the financial ability of the purchaser. At this point the agent should determine if the buyer wishes to involve someone else in the final decision. This can be determined by asking the following:

Mr. and Ms. Jones, it is not uncommon for a family such as yours, looking for the type of home in which you are interested, to want to consult with someone else before making the final decision to buy. When we find the ideal home for you and your family, do you feel that you will make this decision independently or will you want to consult with someone else first?

In asking this question, the agent has an opportunity to determine if such a situation exists. If it does, the agent can attempt to involve this third party in looking at houses with the buyers. Though this is not always going to be possible, at least through this effort one can determine if the buyer might take this course of action and prescribe a potential solution to the problem. When a third party accompanies the buyer during the showings, the agent should be certain not to ignore him or her and involve him or her in everything. This person will be a primary source of advice for the buyer. If left out of part of the showing process, he or she will not be in as good a position to give favorable advice. The third party should be given every consideration extended to the buyer.

If the third party is unwilling to look at houses with the buyer, there is not much one can do. At least the agent has taken a prudent course of action. One school of thought suggests that the mention of this other party may create a problem. The insignificantly few times that this might occur is not enough to negate the tremendous number of times when one can avoid a problem by having the third party accompany the buyer.

ENSURING PROSPECT LOYALTY

How disheartening it is to drive up to a home that an agent wants to show and have the buyer remark, "Oh, we've already seen this one." Not only does it eliminate a home from the agent's list, but also it indicates the involvement of another agent. One of the greatest accomplishments of an agent is generating loyalty from buyers. Too often one expects this to be a natural occurrence rather than a nurtured one. One must understand that buyers do not have a loyalty to anyone exceeding their loyalty to themselves. This is not only true, but the way it should be. A buyer is looking for a home for himself or herself and his or her family; that is the buyer's most important objective. While the buyer might like the agent and be inclined to want to look at homes with that agent, his or her inclination is only that, an inclination. If another agent comes along with a house that's perfect, no buyer is going to refuse to see it.

Buyers don't feel that they have done anything incorrect (which certainly they have not). Since they never indicated that they would do differently, they feel little, if any, remorse in looking at homes with more than one agent. This problem is created by the agent because the agent generally makes no attempt to get the buyers to commit themselves to looking with only one agent. There is a fear that one cannot expect this. If one spends a great deal of time in locating the right home for a family — and it does require a great deal of time — an agent has every right to know what to expect from the buyer.

The agent is always free to decide with whom he or she wishes to work. Buyers who agree to work with only one agent deserve more effort than one who wants to work with many agents. If the buyer has the choice as to how many agents with which to work, the agent should have a choice too.

In attempting to obtain this commitment from the buyer, the agent can take an easy course of action. Following the qualification interview (which can easily last 1½ to 2 hours), some rapport has been generated between buyers and agent. At this point, the agent can pause and ask the buyer the following.

> *Mr. and Ms. Jones, I have an excellent idea of what you are looking for in your new home. All I have is my time and I will spend all the time necessary in locating this home for you, if you will spend all the time that you look at homes with me. If you wish to look on your own or look with other agents as well, I can only afford to work with you in my spare time. Would you prefer that I work for you full-time or part-time?*

This is a very up-front and honest representation of what is necessary to maximize the relationship between the agent and the buyer.

The usual answer is, "OK, we'll give you a couple of weeks and see how you do" or "We'll work exclusively with you; we don't want to go into personal areas of our financial life with others." With these kinds of answers, the agent knows that there is some sense of obligation. This doesn't mean that they won't violate this agreement, but at least the agreement exists. On occasion the agent may have someone refuse to make this commitment. The buyers want to have as many people working for them as possible. The agent knows what his or her position is. The buyers who are looking at houses exclusively with an agent get called first by the agent and those who would not make the commitment of exclusivity are called last.

LAST-MINUTE DETAILS

Prior to leaving the house and after thanking the buyers for their time, there is one last area to be covered with the buyers. If a home comes to their attention from a source other than the agent, they can contact the agent, and he or she will be happy to investigate it for them. Example:

> During your travels around the city or while reading the newspaper should a sign or an ad on a home catch your attention, if you will note the address of the property, I can find out all the details for you, whether it is offered by a REALTOR® or an owner.

Having said this prior to leaving the house, the agent knows that at least there is a chance that the buyers will follow this suggestion (which is almost nonexistent if not suggested).

AFTER-QUALIFICATION FOLLOW-UP

Following the qualification interview the agent enters a very delicate area for the future relationship with the buyers. After the visit to the buyers' home, the buyers' are looking for action. They are expecting results, or they will seek another REALTOR®. The agent should be in touch with the buyers no less than *once per day*. Even if all the agent has to tell the buyer is, "I'm sorry to report that nothing has come on the market today which is in keeping with what you want, but I'll be back in touch tomorrow." The old adage of "no news is good news" does not apply.

Immediately following the qualification interview, the agent should send thank-you notes to the buyers. This is merely an extra effort to help cement the relationship between agent and buyer. The note should be brief and express the agent's appreciation for the confidence that the buyer has expressed in the agent by allowing the agent the opportunity to locate the buyers' new home. This goes a long way and becomes part of the positive impression that the buyers carry.

The qualification interview prior to the showing of property is ideal. There will be times when the agent must show the buyer homes immediately and taking time to prequalify becomes impossible. While this is all part of the need to be flexible, the qualification interview must take place. If it cannot occur before showing the buyer property, then certainly shortly afterward. In no way can an agent be of any significant assistance to any buyer without a qualifying interview.

Exercise

Write a sample dialogue between agent and buyer, illustrating the areas of inquiry during the qualification interview as mentioned in this chapter.

13

Selecting and Showing the Property

After reviewing the information from the qualifying interview, the agent should proceed in locating the homes most consistent with the buyer's requirements. After locating these homes, time should be taken to preview them to determine their acceptability. Only after personally inspecting each property can the agent intelligently and accurately describe the houses to the buyer and show the houses effectively. It is important to attempt to locate homes satisfying as many of the requirements as possible and always satisfying the dominant buying motive.

PREPARING THE PROPERTIES TO BE SHOWN

Before a house is shown, it should be put in its best possible condition. While there are some areas (paint, etc.) that one cannot immediately correct, other areas (messy rooms, etc.) can be altered. The agent should request that the seller prepare the house to be shown. When this isn't or can't be done (sellers out of town, another company's listing, etc.), the agent showing the house should go by the house prior to showing to "set the stage." A list of items such as the tips to get top dollar for your house (Chapter 8) will facilitate this. The agent should also ask the sellers to leave during each showing. Buyers will always spend more time in a home if the seller is not present.

In addition to presenting the house in a neat and clean

condition, the house should appeal to all the senses. It should look, smell, sound, feel, and, yes, even taste pleasant.

Look Pleasant

All lights within the house should be on, not just the main lights but all lamps, oven and range lights, lights in closets, lights in the garage, etc. Every house looks better when brightly lit. In addition all drapes should be open, allowing the sunlight to enhance the beauty of the house.

Smell Pleasant

Houses have a way of giving off musty odors at times. Regardless of such an odor, the house should sprayed with a deodorizer prior to all showings. Sensitivity to odors varies; what seems odor-free to one person may not be to another.

Sound Pleasant

Stereo or radio music should be played during showings to add a soothing touch. The grocery and department store industries have spent a fortune discovering that soft, soothing background music causes people to shop longer.

Feel Pleasant

A house clean and free of dust allows buyers to look at and touch items within houses without picking up unsightly dust and dirt, which certainly would not enhance the experience.

Taste Pleasant

A bottle of chilled mineral or purified water in the refrigerator of the homes being shown is a nice touch. The agent is not only able to offer the customers something to drink but can soothe their thirst with a pleasant quencher (other beverages are fine, but nothing alcoholic should ever be used). The seller should be asked to provide this.

ORDER AND QUANTITY TO SHOW

The question of how many houses to show is always a concern of sales agents, who recognize that buyers can become weary from looking at homes. Therefore, one must be sensitive to wear and tear on the buyers.

Ideally, the agent should show houses in groups of four. The order is not as significant as the continuous qualifying that should occur during the showings. Frequently agents discover additional information during the actual showings of the properties.

Agents develop preferences for the showing order of homes selected for the buyer. Some prefer to show the best houses first and some vice versa. I have always preferred to show the best last (that is, the best of each group of four), due to the purchaser's desire to see all houses selected for showing. If they fall in love with the first house, they will generally want to see the rest before they make a decision.

Every buyer should be given a list of the pertinent information about each house and something on which to make notes. If the agent takes the information from the listing and puts it on a legal-size page (one for each house), there will be plenty of room for notes on each page. One should encourage the buyers to make notes about each house.

There are numerous advantages to showing houses in groups of four. One can control the showings and keep the buyers from getting confused with too many houses. After the first four houses the agent and buyers should take a break and have a cup of coffee or lunch. During this time, the agent should ask the buyers to rate the four houses. After this, one should ask what facet of the first-rated house caused it to be rated number 1. In doing this, the customer and agent can eliminate 75 percent of what has been shown. If for some reason the buyers can't decide on a number 1, the agent should reshow the houses so that they make a decision. (If they can't pick one of four, they won't be able to do so from eight either.) After the rating and discussion of the first group, the agent should proceed to the second group.

After showing the second group of four homes, the agent should suggest another break, perhaps for a cold drink. During this pause, a rating should be requested of the houses. The agent should then find out how house 1 in the second group compares to house 1 in the first group. The buyers must decide which one they prefer and why. If they can't, the agent should reshow the two top-rated houses. The objective is to allow the buyer to view property and make small decisions about desirability. This not only allows the agent an opportunity to learn more about what the buyer wants but also narrows the area of consideration.

The agent should continue this process until the buyers have found the home that they want or until the homes selected for showing are exhausted. At that point the agent should reshow the top-rated houses and allow the buyers to decide on one of those homes (assuming that the homes met the areas discussed in the qualification interview).

Agents who utilize this method of showing houses find that they can eliminate an enormous amount of time showing buyers homes. There is no magic number of houses to show to a family. One wants to show as few as possible, but different buyers require different numbers. When dealing with people, one can't generalize and show only *x* number of houses and expect a decision. One can, however, have a plan of showing houses in groupings. This gives the greatest opportunity to reach a sale within the most reasonable time.

ROUTE TO THE PROPERTY

Ideally, the houses to be shown will be in an order that literally allows the agent to go from one house to the next, without backtracking (though backtracking is sometimes unavoidable).

In any case, one should take the most attractive and pleasant route to the property. Though one always wants to minimize the amount of time spent driving from one house to another, a few extra minutes of driving time that allow the agent to show the buyers the amenities within the neighborhood (swimming pools, parks, playgrounds, tennis courts, shopping, etc.) are very valuable.

PREPARING THE BUYERS

Prior to showing any house, the agent should advise the buyers that the sellers have gone to a lot of trouble to get their homes ready to be shown. If any of the homes at first glance does not appear to be exactly what the buyers are looking for, they should give the seller the courtesy of looking at the house. This technique prevents resistance to seeing houses whose exteriors aren't attractive to the buyer.

WHAT TO DO UPON ARRIVAL

Upon arriving at the property, the agent should park across the street from the house to allow the buyer the full view of the property. The purchaser should always enter the house through the front door. If the agent has a key to the house's back door, the buyers should wait at the front door while the agent enters the house. This is suggested because the first impression of the home is important.

When entering through the same door, the agent should always enter the property first. Though the polite gesture is to open the door and allow the customers to enter first, this is a potentially hazardous method of showing houses. These are strange houses to the buyers. Even if a home is vacant, buyers are timid about walking into other people's homes.

TAKING BUYERS THROUGH THE PROPERTY

As the agent shows the house to the buyers, the buyers should accept the house room by room. Therefore the buyers should be guided through the home, and the agent should maintain the buyer's attention to the room being shown at the time and not rush through or minimize any room in the house.

PIQUING THE BUYERS' INTEREST

In an effort to involve the buyers in the property, the agent should ask questions of the buyers as they look through each house. To take the buyers through the home and do the usual "This is the kitchen, this is the bathroom, this is the master bedroom," etc., makes the experience of looking at houses mundane and generally uninteresting. Through thought-provoking questions, the buyers become more interested. Some examples are:

> *Ms. Jones, how do you feel your furniture would look best in the family room?*
>
> *Would you keep your tools in the garage or the storage room?*
>
> *Which cabinets would you use for china and which for your crystal?*

How would these colors coordinate with your furniture?

Which bedroom would be your son's room and which your daughter's?

These questions involve the customers throughout the showings and cause them to think about things ordinarily put off until seeing many houses and being reshown the houses liked best.

RECOGNIZING BUYING SIGNALS

During the showings of houses buyers will give certain clues as to their hidden interests in a home or homes. If the agent is aware of this, it is beneficial.

Buying signals usually center around questions that only someone interested in the property would ask. While the degree of the interest is something the agent must develop, the indications are identifiable. Some examples and suggested responses follow.

BUYER: *What do you think the sellers would take for the house?*

AGENT: *All that I know is that they will accept the listed price. How much is the house worth to you?*

BUYER: *Do the drapes stay with the house?*

AGENT: *Do you want the drapes? or Would you like the house if they did?*

BUYER: *How soon do they want to be out of the house?*

AGENT: *How soon would you like to be in?*

BUYER: *Are the sellers going to paint the house before they leave?*

AGENT: *Would you like the house painted? Would you like the house if they did?*

BUYER: *Will the seller participate in the financing?*

AGENT: *To what extent would you like them to?*

In these examples, one can see that these questions are unnecessary if the buyers do not like the house. Why would one be interested in what remains with a home or how soon the sellers need to vacate unless interested in the property? These questions and similar ones, only asked by someone interested in a property, are buying signals. The agent must be keenly aware of their existence in an effort to know when to probe further into the buyers' interest in any one particular home.

CONTROLLING THE BUYERS

As the agent shows houses to the buyers, the agent should always strive to keep husband and wife together. If they go in different directions, control is completely lost. Therefore, if the husband wants to see the garage and the wife is interested in the kitchen, the agent should ask the husband to accompany the wife to the kitchen and then all go to see the garage. This is, of course, not always possible, but it is important to try. In keeping the buyers together, the agent has the opportunity of having all the parties present as points about each room are brought out and can avoid reshowing homes for the benefit of the one not present in a particular part of the house.

Exercise

What can you do to prepare a home to be shown?

List 10 examples of what you feel could be labeled as buying signals.

14

Handling Objections and Closing the Sale

As is always the case with communication, attempting to understand the motive and meaning behind the buyer's objection will prove enormously beneficial in dealing with the objection. As pointed out in Chapter 7, during the discussion on the seller's objections, there are basically two types of objections: an objection stemming purely from sales resistance and an objection to a condition. An objection from sales resistance (the unconscious tendency to resist being sold) and one from a condition (something that makes the house wrong for the buyer due to an undesirable condition, i.e., a family who wants a family room objecting to the lack of one) must be identified by the agent in order to handle the problem properly.

OBJECTIONS STEMMING FROM SALES RESISTANCE

These types of objections are presented to agents frequently by customers. They are easily identifiable; they are generally not asked by people who have no interest in what they are being shown. Objections stemming from sales resistance will generally carry with them validation for the home in general (i.e., a couple objecting to the size of a guest room that will not be used more than two or three times a year at the most; such an objection wouldn't be made unless they liked the house in general). As a result, the agent must tactfully overcome the potential problem since these objections don't generally have any firm basis.

OBJECTIONS TO A CONDITION

These types of objections differ entirely from those stemming from sales resistance. These objections generally develop when the buyer is shown the wrong house. The previous example about a couple who wants a family room and objects to the lack of one in a house being shown, supports this position. Trying to show a family a house deficient in a need expressed by the buyers is to set oneself up for failure. The agent's job is to show people houses satisfying the needs, wants, and desires of their families and within their financial ability.

The preceding example of an objection to a condition comes from a couple with the financial wherewithal to afford a home with a family room, but the agent has chosen to show them a home without one, thus resulting in an objection to the condition. If the buyer could not afford a home with a family room and the agent had suggested to the family considering something smaller, more in the desired price range, and they agreed, the showing of such a house would have been in order; perhaps the objection at that point would have stemmed from sales resistance. Knowledge of the previous discusions between the agent and the buyer is essential in making the final determination as to what kind of an objection the agent is dealing with.

FIVE STEPS TO OVERCOME OBJECTIONS

The same five-step process (Chapter 7) to overcoming a sellers' objection can be applied to handling buyers' objections:

1. Listen attentively
2. Acknowledge the customer's point of view
3. Qualify the objection
4. Answer the objection
5. Close

One must (1) listen attentively to be sure that he or she has heard and understands the nature of the objection; (2) acknowledge that the customer has every right to feel that way; (3) make sure that the expressed objection is all that the customer feels and that he or she isn't failing to express anything else; (4) give a complete and logical answer to the objection that is satisfactory to the customer; and (5) get the customer to make a positive decision. An example follows.

Earlier, a couple had objected that the guest room was too small. As background information, this couple had told the agent during the qualifying interview that a requirement for their new home was a guest room so that the children would not have to room together when the grandmother made her annual visit. The grandmother never stayed more than four or five days and was rarely in the room other than to sleep. The room would probably not be used by anyone else during the year other than an unexpected house guest once or twice. The agent had determined that the couple's dominant buying motive is having their children attend the finest schools, which the location of this house will satisfy. Based on the qualifying interview, the agent believes this house to be ideal for this family.

The agent treats this objection as one stemming from sales resistance and handles it as follows.

BUYER: *(After looking at the home a second time) The guest room is too small.*

AGENT: *(After listening to the objection and waiting for the buyer to express any additional concerns) I understand how you feel and I'm sure that if it weren't for the size of the guest room, you'd invest in this house tonight, wouldn't you?*

BUYER: *Yes, we would.*

AGENT: *As you indicated, this room will be used for only a few days a year, and you had said everything else about the house was perfect. Mr. and Mrs. Jones, I know that you want your children to attend the finest schools, so isn't it true that the size of the guest room is less important than the quality of education your children receive?*

BUYER: *That's true, and I'm sure grandmother won't care, as little as she is in the room.*

AGENT: *Did you want to use $10,000 or $15,000 as earnest money?*

BUYER: *$10,000, and we want to move in immediately after taking title to the property.*

TYPICAL OBJECTIONS

In an effort to avoid redundancy, this section only addresses itself to possible answers (step 4) for overcoming objections from the buyer:

Objection 1:   *The house needs some work before we would consider it.*

In this situation, the buyer has indicated that the house is fine if some work were done. If the house weren't right the buyer would never have mentioned the work. The agent should attempt to ascertain exactly what work needs to be done, the cost of performing this work, and, if the buyer will not pay for the work, try to negotiate this amount with the seller.

Objection 2:   *The price is too high.*

Based on the qualifying interview, the agent knows that the buyer can afford the home. This is not an objection centering around an inability to pay, but rather an amount more than the buyer wants to pay or thinks he or she should pay.

The agent should submit to the buyer a market analysis showing the prices of houses in the area. In this way the buyer can truly appreciate the value of the home in question. If this is not sufficient to justify the price being asked for the home, the agent should relate the house to others that the buyers have seen that are comparably priced but do not compare in quality and features.

Frequently, such comments come in the form of sales resistance or the desire for a better buy on the home.

Objection 3:   *Interest rates are too high.*

While at times this is a real concern of buyers, one should first attempt to come up with alternative forms of financing so that, by virtue of the sellers' participating in the financing, the buyer might bypass conventional mortgage rates. Usually, if the buyer is willing to offer the seller more money for the house, the sellers will take a lower rate of interest on the note that they are being asked to hold.

Aside from this option, with inflation and appreciating homes values (if one is in an area appreciating in value) by the time interest rates decline to what the buyer feels are more acceptable, the price of the home that the buyer wants might increase so that the delay wasn't worthwhile. In the case of many different types of mortgages, rates are reviewed every few years. If there is a substantial decline in interest rates after the purchase, the buyer's rate would ultimately be adjusted.

When interest rates become so high that they cause a massive slowdown in the housing industry, particularly new construction, there is potential for enormous inflation in the price of existing housing. When interest rates drop to a more palatable level, there is a tremendous increase in the number of buyers entering the marketplace. With an inadequate number of new homes to fill this need and with at least 12 months necessary for the new home supply to catch up with demand, buyers have only one alternative: the existing housing market. When demand exceeds supply, prices increase. In this situation, houses increase in price astronomically and clearly justify the necessity to invest in housing when one has the need rather than being concerned with interest rates and delaying a purchase in hopes of declining mortgage rates.

Additionally, when high interest rates become part of the economic way of life, they are part of how business is done. If one wants a new home, and rates are higher than in the past, that must be accepted. In most parts of the country it has rarely been more advantageous to a buyer to wait to buy because of interest rates, when the buyer was faced with the alternative of renting.

Objection 4:   *Taxes on this house are too high.*

They are too high compared to what? If the tax rate in an area is higher than the buyer is used to, that should have been expected. The buyer is looking for a certain kind of home because the buyer wants what the home has to offer; the home has a tax rate consistent with its type. Therefore, tax rates should be viewed much the way as utility bills when a couple is going from a smaller home to a larger one. It is part of the related cost of owning such a home.

Objection 5:   *We'd like to see more houses.*

This statement must be examined by the agent in order to determine the true motive behind the buyers' comment. If the agent feels that the home being shown to the buyers is everything that the buyers have indicated that they wanted, there is a possibility that this is merely an effort to avoid making a decision. The agent must ascertain what improvements in other houses would be more desirable than what has been seen. This gives the agent additional information to decide the next course of action. If the additional features are in fact lacking in the houses already seen, the agent should note that and show additional houses.

If the buyers offer little in the way of additional features and merely want to look at more, the agent is faced with two courses of action. First, the agent, sensitive to the fact that buyers often feel that they should see many houses before making a decision, should point out to the buyers that it is common to find the right home in the initial stages of looking. The agent is trained to find the right home for the buyer quickly, which is the reason for the qualification interview. After establishing this, the agent should again attempt to close. If the agent finds the buyers not interested in making a decision so quickly, he or she should try to determine what the buyers feel would be an adequate selection. In doing this, the agent attempts to cause the buyers to think in terms of finding a house from *x* number instead of looking at an endless number of homes. The agent should, with great courtesy, show additional homes to the buyers, always referring to the home that the buyers liked but on which avoided making a decision. Ideally, one will have to show no more than four additional properties. This is never a desirable situation to encounter, but it must be dealt with. If the buyers sense a reluctance on the part of the agent to show additional houses, it may cause a serious breakdown in rapport and loss of trust. It must be handled delicately.

Objection 6:   *This certainly isn't much compared to the house we had before.*

With the great mobility in our society, we are seeing more and more of this when dealing with buyers. Though some areas are experiencing the opposite and buyers are elated with how much house they are getting for the money, frequently we are seeing buyers upset with what they will have to settle for in the new community. The agent can do nothing but sympathize with the buyers. If the buyers want to stay in the price range the agent is showing, they will have to look at that type of home. If the buyers would like to invest more money, the agent can show larger homes.

Objection 7:   *We wanted a larger lot.*

The first thing that the agent must determine is the reason for the larger lot. If it is just for appearance, it can be overcome more easily than if the buyers want to add a pool. If for appearance, one can point out that a larger lot is more expensive, or, to stay in the same price range, means a smaller house. Another consideration is that a small lot requires less care and therefore affords a family more leisure time.

In the case of a future pool, the agent may be asking the buyers to forego a long-range goal and, at best, cause them to sell this home in order to get a pool. This may not be desirable at all and require showing houses with larger lots.

Objection 8:   *This house is probably the smallest home in the area. We'd prefer to have a home that is more typical of the area in which we live.*

Assuming that the house in question is in the price range of the buyers, this means that all other houses are probably more expensive. There is a very real advantage to being the least expensive house on the block. The house appreciates faster than the others and will always sell faster. Owning the least expensive house is a very desirable position. Besides, if this house were like the others in the area, it would be more expensive and, if it were in an area of similar houses, it would be in a less expensive neighborhood.

Objection 9:   *We're not used to a busy street, and the noise of the passing cars would drive us crazy.*

This is a common complaint from people who have never lived on heavily traveled streets. If the home is perfect and no other problems exist, the agent might mention that, after living in a house exposed to consistent street noises, the people in the houses frequently develop an immunity to the noise. People who live on busy streets rarely complain about the noise of the traffic. They tune it out. (A good example is how we fail to notice the noise of an air conditioner until asked to listen for it.)

Objection 10:   *I'd like my lawyer to review the contract before I sign.*

While this comment means a delay in the presentation of the offer to the seller, this is a real and understandable desire. A contract to invest in property is a legal document; if the buyer does not feel comfortable in entering into such an agreement without first consulting an attorney, so be it. The agent must make every attempt to go with the buyer to the attorney's office to answer any questions from the attorney. Attorneys are a real part of the sale of real estate; agents should make every attempt to work closely and harmoniously with them.

WHEN TO PERSIST AND WHEN TO BACK OFF

The preceding suggestions are merely that, suggestions. Every situation is different; not all techniques work in all cases. Agents must remain aware of what is happening. Does a situation exist where the buyers have little if any reason to postpone a decision; are they tired and don't want to consider the decision any longer? Only the agent can sense this and then may not always be right.

The best tactic is to be persistent about what one feels is the right thing for the buyer to do and always be sensitive to whether the buyer is remaining receptive to the agent's direction. If it is sensed that the buyer is becoming hostile, the agent must ease off. Few people say *yes* because they are asked to buy. Successful salespeople are persistent but work at keeping their antenna up for the moment when they must back off. Knowing which to do and when is an acquired ability, one that will eventually come to the agent who works at developing this sixth sense.

CLOSING THE SALE

In every selling situation, there comes a time when the salesperson must suggest that the customer buy what is being considered. The agent's effort is considered *closing the sale*. Often salespeople have difficulties in bringing up the subject of buying, but if this is not initiated by the salesperson, the buyer may not make the decision at all. One must recognize that there are benefits to asking for the sale regardless of the outcome. If the buyer buys, the benefits are obvious. If the buyers refuses, the salesperson knows that objections must be dealt with or that the salesperson has taken the buyer to the wrong house. In either case, the salesperson becomes more aware of the buyer's attitude than without the attempt to close the sale.

During our discussion on closing the listing (Chapter 8), we had established that one should appeal to the seller's logic. Closing techniques, as well as all other techniques, must be void of any form of manipulation, or the salesperson will severely damage rapport. This is also true when dealing with the buyer. Our earlier discussion suggested six different closing techniques, all useful in dealing with the buyer.

Yes/Yes Close

This closing technique gives the buyer a choice between two courses of action, either of which is acceptable, such as:

> Mr. and Mrs. Buyer, would you like to take occupancy on the 1st or the 15th?

This gives the buyers a choice between two dates for occupancy of the home, either of which means that they will buy. Others might be, "Would you like to apply for an 80 percent or 90 percent mortgage?" or "Would you prefer to have the house on the cul-de-sac or the one with the pool?"

In every case, the buyer is given a choice between two alternatives, which are both positive actions toward buying.

Positive/Negative Close

In an attempt to present the facts to the buyers so that they may weigh the positives against the negatives, this technique proves most beneficial with many buyers, particularly those who want to think it over.

AGENT:	*Mr. and Mrs. Buyer, as I understand it, you are concerned about making the proper decision, is that correct?*
BUYERS:	*That is absolutely right.*
AGENT:	*Let me make a suggestion that helps a lot of my customers. Whenever I deal with someone in your position, I find that usually if it is the right thing to do, the facts will speak for themselves. Let's take a piece of paper and pencil (agent takes out a pencil and paper) and divide it in half (agent draws a line down the center of the paper). On the left side we'll put a plus and on the right side a minus (agent writes a plus and minus on the appropriate sides). In the plus column we will list all the reasons for making a positive decision and in the minus column we will list all the reasons for making a negative decision. When we finish, we will total the columns, and the decision will be made. (The agent hands the pen and paper to the customer.) Why don't we try it?*

Through this technique, the buyers can weigh positive aspects of the purchase against negatives (which they may have allowed to get out of proportion). Any important decision should be reached using a method that compares positives to negatives; the investment in a home is definitely an important decision. At this point the agent's role becomes one of a counselor. The agent should assist the buyer in determining as many positives as possible but to allow the buyers to determine their own negatives.

This procedure is followed since the buyer will comment to the contrary if a positive mentioned by the agent is not viewed by the buyer as a positive. However, negatives cannot be readily expressed by anyone other than the buyer. It would be foolish for the agent to suggest problems not presenting themselves as such to the buyer.

Comparison Closes

The two structures discussed in Chapter 8 were:

> *I know that you want (positive) , so isn't it true that (negative) is less important than (positive) ?*

> *While (negative) seems vital at this moment, in the long run your ability to (positive) dominates your decision, doesn't it?*

As an alternative to the positive/negative close, when a customer is perhaps allowing a negative to become a bigger obstacle than it really is, this technique compares what the customer wants to achieve and what he or she views as a problem. An example might be one discussed earlier in which the buyers were concerned with the size of a guest room to be used only once or twice a year. Knowing that the buyers are interested in one of the benefits of the property, the schools that their children will be attending, the agent might use one of the following approaches:

> *Mr. and Mrs. Jones, I know that you want your children to attend the finest schools, so isn't it true that the size of the guest room is less important than the quality of education that your children receive?*

> *While the size of the guest room seems vital at this moment, in the long run your ability to have your children attend these fine schools really dominates your decision, doesn't it?*

Similar Situation Close

This technique can be most effective if one uses a great deal of tact.

Relating actual situations that have occurred to others in the same situation as the buyer is certainly a method of showing the buyer, indirectly, possible gains or losses.

For example, in the situation where a buyer could afford to invest in a new home before the old home has sold but is leaning toward waiting for the home to sell, the obvious danger is that the home that the buyer wants may sell before the buyer's home sells. If this occurs, there is the problem of starting to look for homes all over again. While the buyer could deal with this, it is ridiculous to do so after finding the desired home. Pointing out this fact is not always as effective as relating a similar situation that occurred to someone else.

> *Mr. and Ms. Seller, while I can well appreciate your desire to sell your home before investing in this home, there is something that you should consider. What happens if this home sells before your home sells? I dealt with a buyer not long ago in the same position and though we had found the ideal home for him and his family, he wanted to wait to sell his home. As fate would have it, the home that he wanted sold before his did, and we had to start over looking at homes. Though we did find another home, it wasn't quite as special as the one that got away. I know that you don't want to run that risk, do you?*

This situation must be true. If an agent hasn't had such an experience, he or she must find an agent in the office who has and get the name and phone number of the party. If there is any question as to the validity of the story, the agent must be prepared to furnish the name and phone number of the individual.

Cushion

Another way of expressing a similar situation could be with the use of the *cushion*. The cushion incorporates the use of the words *feel*, *felt*, and *found*. For example:

> *Ms. Jones, I know how you feel. Last year I had a customer who felt much the way you do. She found that had she immediately invested in the new home that she wanted instead of waiting for her home to sell, she would have avoided the loss of that new home to another buyer.*

Order-Blank Close

The application of this close is wide and varied. At the appropriate moment, when the agent feels that the buyer should make a positive decision about buying a home, and in the absence of any affirmative actions on the part of the buyer, this technique can be used most effectively.

This technique requires the agent to start completing the contract. Often this simple action is actually a welcome relief for the buyer. In completing the contract to purchase, the agent should ask the buyer questions relating to the purchase of the property, such as "You had mentioned that you wanted to be in the house as soon as possible. What if we asked for possession on the day of the closing?" and "How do you feel about asking the sellers to make a decision on this offer within 24 hours?"

These questions are necessary in order to make a positive decision about investing. Until the buyers stop the agent, they have indicated their approval. If they raise a question about the actions of the agent, the agent should respond honestly and point out that these were important points to determine before presenting an offer to the seller. This opens up discussion regarding the writing of an offer and can be only beneficial.

When the agreement to purchase is signed, the agent must give the purchaser a Net Sheet (Figure 14-1) which itemizes all costs related to the purchase of the home. This is done in an attempt to make the purchaser as aware as possible of all anticipated expenses to avoid hidden surprises.

A WORD ABOUT EARNEST MONEY

Basically, earnest money is, in addition to an expression of good faith on the part of the buyer, a sum of money that can accomplish two real objectives: (1) remove the buyer from the marketplace and (2) in the event of default on the part of the buyer, compensate the seller for any loss experienced by having removed the house from the market while the buyer arranged financing.

The amount of earnest money put with an offer to purchase has long been debated. While the amount of earnest money is not important after the sale has been closed, it must be viewed as to what can, and often does, occur prior to the closing of the sale.

Removing the Buyer from the Marketplace

When a buyer uses a small amount of money as an earnest money deposit with an offer to purchase, it is usually not sufficient to deter the buyer from considering other properties. While the buyer may not be actively pursuing other properties after making an offer to purchase, one must consider the number of other agents or sellers with whom the buyer had contact prior to this offer. The question is, what would the buyer do if a beautiful home that the buyer had seen came available at a bargain price and with irresistible terms, after the buyer made an offer to purchase another home and that offer was accepted? Most probably, if the amount of earnest money were small, the buyer might well forego it in order to take advantage of this new opportunity.

A sufficient amount of money would most probably prevent such an occurrence. While the buyer might choose to invest in both houses and resell or rent one, the transaction would be consummated in an effort to save the earnest money.

Compensating the Seller for Buyer Default

In the preceding situation when the buyer placed a small amount of earnest money with an offer to purchase and chose to buy another house and forfeit the earnest money, what happens to the seller? In many cases, the seller gains $500 or $1,000 and loses any number of other buyers while the house was off the market during preparations for closing.

This timeframe can often be four to six weeks or more. Often one of the busiest times of the year has passed, and the seller must return the house to the market at a less favorable time. Frequently the sellers, anticipating the closing of the transaction, will move out of the house and into their new home and must put an unfurnished house on the market. Since furnished houses generally sell for more than vacant ones, this further impairs their potential for a good price.

Obtaining Sufficient Earnest Money

While there is no guarantee that any transaction will close, collecting a sufficient amount of earnest money can reduce the possibilities of this dilemma. A good rule of thumb is to collect 5 percent of

PROPERTY ADDRESS _____

SALES PRICE _____

TERMS _____

LOAN AMT. _____

INT. RATE _____

POINTS _____

PURCHASER	SELLER
LOAN ORIGINATION FEE	
APPROX. LOAN DISCOUNT (%)	
PRIVATE MORTGAGE INSURANCE (PMI)	
APPRAISAL FEE	
ATTORNEY'S FEE (DEED AND LOAN PAPERS)	
PHOTOS	
APPLICATION FEE	
TRANSFER FEE	
GUARANTEED TITLE INSURANCE POLICY	
MORTGAGEE'S TITLE POLICY	
ESCROW FEE	
CERTIFIED COPY OF RESTRICTIONS	
RECORDING FEE (DEED OF TRUST, REL., DEED)	
TAX CERTIFICATES	
SURVEY	
TERMITE INSPECTION	
MECHANICAL INSPECTIONS	
REALTOR'S FEE	
TOTAL	

182

PREPAID ITEMS ESTIMATE

Maintenance	
FHA Mortgage Ins. ( ) Mo	
Hazard Ins. Premium ( ) Yr.	
Hazard Ins. Deposit ( ) Mos.	
Advance Taxes ( ) Mos.	
Interim Int. $ ___ Per Day	
0 – 30 Days Estimated Days	
TOTAL	

MONTHLY PAYMENT ESTIMATE

Principal and Interest	
Taxes	
Hazard Insurance	
Other Insurance (FHA, Flood, Etc.)	
Maintenance	
ESTIMATED PAYMENT	

ESTIMATED TOTAL MONEY NEEDED AT CLOSING

Down Payment	
Closing Costs	
Prepaid Items	
Sub Total	
Less: Earnest Money	
DUE AT CLOSING	

ESTIMATE OF AMOUNT DUE SELLER

Sale Price	
Plus: Escrow Return	
Sub Total	
Less: Loan Balance	
Closing Costs	
Prepayment Pen.	
Interest and Taxes	
Sub Total	
APPROX. NET	

Figure 14-1.   Net Sheet

the sale price or $2,500, whichever is greater. In case of government-insured loans, which may ultimately require the buyer to close the transaction with less total cash than $2,500 or 5 percent, the agent should request the buyers put as earnest money all the monies needed for closing the transaction. They must come up with the money sooner or later; they may as well do so at this time. Transactions with total cash requirements in excess of this suggested amount should not prove any problem.

In either case, it is merely a matter of asking for the amount desired rather than accepting whatever the buyer offers. Buyers will generally follow the request of the agent if they are given the reasons for putting up more money. While the reasons for a sufficient amount of earnest money to accompany the offer are numerous, the buyer is only interested in those which are in his or her best interest. Following are some valid suggestions that can be presented to the buyer in different situations.

Often the direct approach is all that is needed — simply ask the buyer for the desired amount of earnest money:

> Mr. Jones, we're going to offer $80,000; would you like to include $4,000 or $5,000 earnest money?

When an offer is less than list price, the agent can point out to the buyer how a generous amount of earnest money can be to his advantage:

> Mr. and Mrs. Buyer, you are asking that the seller accept an amount less than they have indicated they will accept. My experience has been that sellers are much more encouraged when they see a substantial amount of earnest money with the offer.

When a house has been shown frequently, the agent can show how earnest money can make the buyer's offer more attractive than others that might be received:

> Mr. Jones, this particular home is being seen by a great many buyers. If an offer comes in at the same time as yours, they must be presented together. Sellers will always lean toward the offer that looks the best, and earnest money makes an offer attractive.

If another agent is going to present the offer to the seller, it can be useful to point out this person's influence on the seller:

> Mr. Buyer, the listing agent is going to present this offer to the seller, and I can assure you that the agent is very

experienced and will encourage the seller to request more earnest money. You run the risk of another offer coming in before you can consider the seller's counteroffer for more earnest money, and could lose the house.

When the buyers say they don't currently have all the earnest money, the agent must suggest other sources that the buyer might approach for additional funds (i.e., relatives, friends, stock sale, etc.). If the buyers indicate that they can come up with more money but will need a few days, the agent should indicate a total amount of earnest money payable in terms meeting with the situation of the buyer, for instance, $4,000 total earnest money with $1,000 payable at the time and the balance on or before ten days (or however many days is acceptable) from the date of the contract. This allows the buyer to buy and the seller to be assured that the property will not be tied up for a long time with a small amount of earnest money.

When buyers don't want to put up sufficient earnest money because of losing interest on their funds, the agent must point out that this is just part of the process of buying a home and show them how little actual interest they are losing:

Mr. and Mrs. Buyer, I understand exactly how you feel, and frankly I have felt much the same way myself when buying property. But I found that the amount of interest actually lost due to the early withdrawal was certainly not enough to risk losing the house. You indicated that the additional $4,000 needed for the 30 days until closing was in your credit union at 9% interest. That comes to about $30. Certainly that isn't enough to concern yourself with, is it?

Handling Sellers' Lack of Concern for Earnest Money

While the agent cannot make the decision for the seller, it is the agent's responsibility to advise the seller about what could become a problem. In good conscience, no agent can advise a seller to do that which the agent would not do himself or herself. One must be completely up front with the seller, advise about options, and never be afraid to suggest asking for more earnest money. The agent works for the seller and not the buyer (unless the buyer has agreed to pay the agent a fee exclusive of the seller). If the buyer should not pursue the transaction because the seller wanted a fair amount of earnest money, in all probability the original offer was not a good one. This should always be explained to the seller when deciding to go to the buyer for more earnest money.

Earnest money can be viewed as the main link in the chain. If it is weak, so is the chain.

REASSURING THE BUYERS

Upon execution of the agreement to purchase, the agent must reassure the buyers that they have made a wise decision. Things like buyers' remorse often occur due to a lack of positive feedback following the sale. Since this does not generally come from those individuals close to the buyers, it is wise for the agent to offer his or her reassurance. For example:

> *Mr. and Mrs. Jones, I want to express my sincere congratulations on the decision that you have made today. Based on all the homes that we have seen, this is unquestionably the one that not only best suits your needs but is the best value as well.*

Exercise

Give three examples of uses of the closing techniques discussed in this chapter.

15

Referral Prospecting and Dealing with Lost Sales

Referrals from friends and acquaintances can provide an enormous amount of business, as discussed with people-to-people PR work. Another way of attaining this end is *referral prospecting*, which is designed to obtain referrals from one's customers.

WHEN TO REFERRAL PROSPECT

There are three primary occasions when the agent should ask the buyer for business. They are (1) when the offer to purchase has been accepted, (2) when the buyer's loan has been approved, and (3) when the sale closes. These are mental "highs" for the buyers. They have gained agreement with the sellers on a sale price, they have received the nod from the lender on their loan, and they have taken title to the property. During each of these positive moments an agent can usually get the greatest amount of cooperation from the purchaser. The agent must realize that the failure of a buyer to refer a customer to the agent is not the buyer's fault. It's the agent's for not asking.

PROCEDURE

The agent should carry index cards and be prepared to ask the buyers for the names of four people who might be in the market for a new home. Additionally, one should ask the buyers to indicate their opinions as to priority and to please call the potential customer so

189

that they are expecting the agent's call. If the buyers do this for the agent, there is every possibility that the majority of the names given will work with the agent, usually exclusively. Furthermore, while some will not give the names of anyone, if one asks for names on three different occasions the odds are that on one of those occasions the buyers will give a positive response.

The following is an example of the use of this technique.

AGENT: *(After arriving at the buyer's home to deliver a copy of the executed contract by the seller) Mr. and Mrs. Buyer, I am so pleased for you as I know how perfect that house is for you and your family.*

BUYERS: *Thank you, Mr. Agent, we are very happy.*

AGENT: *May I ask a favor?*

BUYERS: *Of course.*

AGENT: *My livelihood is dependent upon my ability to work with people such as yourselves who are interested in locating a home. Among the people with whom you work, socialize, or perhaps attend church, would you give me the names of four families whom you feel might be interested in locating a new home?*

BUYERS: *Well, Mr. Agent, there is only one name that comes to mind immediately. There is a new lawyer in our office, Mike Jones. He has just moved here from Florida and is bringing his wife and family as soon as they sell their home.*

AGENT: *(Writing the name on an index card) Has Mr. Jones been looking at any homes?*

BUYERS: *I really don't know. I think he was going to wait for his wife to come in this weekend.*

AGENT: · *I really appreciate this suggestion. Anyone else you know?*

BUYERS: *I'll have to think about it. I will let you know if anyone else comes to mind.*

AGENT: *Thanks so much. Would you mind letting Mr. Jones know that I'll be calling tomorrow?*

BUYER: *I'd be happy to.*

In this situation the agent not only obtained a good customer but has laid the groundwork for the buyer to think of recommending the agent in the future. It would be wise of the agent to check back with the buyer in a few days to see if anyone else's name came to mind.

The same kind of procedure should be used following the approval of the loan and the closing of the sale to obtain names of more buyers.

AGENT: *Mr. and Mrs. Buyer, as I've mentioned before, I'm very interested in dealing with other families who need a professional REALTOR®. Is there anyone else whom you would recommend that I contact?*

MS. BUYER: *I did hear of a lady at the tennis club who was going to move. Her name is Ms. Margaret Prospect.*

MR. BUYER: *I have a client who asked me yesterday if I knew a REALTOR® and I told him to contact you and gave him your card.*

AGENT: *That's wonderful. How might I get in touch with Ms. Prospect?*

MS. BUYER: *I have her number in the club roster. Wait and I'll get it for you.*

AGENT: *Mr. Buyer, I appreciate so much your giving my card to your client, but I'm out of the office so much I'd hate to miss his call. May I ask how I might reach him?*

MR. BUYER: *Sure, his name is John Smith and is with the Acme Drilling Company on Fourth Street.*

MS. BUYER: *Here's the number for Margaret. It's 555-1111, and her husband's name is Bill. I think he's a dentist.*

AGENT: *(As he transfers all this information to index cards) Thank you both so much. Do you have any idea as to their timetables?*

MR. BUYER: *All I know is that he asked if I knew a good REALTOR®.*

MS. BUYER: *I believe that Margaret and her husband are returning to California. He has bought a dental practice there and they are moving*

> *to be close to their parents, who are elderly and in poor health.*

AGENT: *I really appreciate it. Ms. Jones, would you mind mentioning our conversation to Ms. Prospect and tell her I'll be calling.*

MS. BUYER: *Certainly, I'll call her this evening.*

In this situation, Mr. Prospect had already mentioned the agent, so there is no need for him to contact the buyer whom he was referring. By the conversation, one can conclude that while Mr. Buyers' referral could be eager to find something, if Ms. Buyer's information is accurate, the Prospects are in immediate need of a REALTOR® and should be contacted immediately.

LOST SALES

Eventually everyone must deal with learning that a customer with whom he or she has been working has bought from someone else. While this is not happy news, in the long run it can prove profitable if handled properly.

When such news is discovered, an agent must maintain composure and tell the buyers that while the agent is sorry that they didn't find the right house together, the agent is glad that they have found a home that they like and hope that they live there in the best of health. At this point there is little else that one can do. Additionally, one must find out which house that they have bought and when they are moving. If one makes an extra effort without being involved in the transaction, perhaps the buyers will feel a sense of obligation and refer a prospective buyer to the agent.

One should send a note to them immediately, expressing best wishes in their new home. This can be followed by a house-warming gift (nothing expensive, a simple plant will do nicely), which should be delivered in person. This presents an opportunity to bring the gift, see the house, and rebuild any damage to rapport as a result of the involvement of another agent. It's not that the other agent had done anything but rather there may be a loss of loyalty merely due to the other agent's involvement. All this takes little effort and expense and can prove most beneficial. At this point how else can one benefit from this lost transaction?

Exercise

Explain the use of referral prospecting and how it should be applied.

16

Obtaining and Presenting the Offer and Counteroffer

Basically, the purchasers should be encouraged to make their best offer to the sellers and not play games in their attempts to negotiate. Though many buyers will have to try, it is rewarding when one finds how many will follow the suggestions of the agent. An estimated cost sheet must be prepared for the buyer to show the estimated total cost of acquiring the house at the offered price. When problems in arriving at a fair price occur, the introduction of the competitive market analysis is extremely beneficial. It shows the buyer how fairly priced the house is and often eliminates much of the buyer's apprehension in making an offer close to the listed price.

What a pleasure it would be if once an offer were made, the agent could simply contact the seller and obtain acceptance. This is rarely the case. Many times the work of getting the house sold really begins once the offer is made by the buyer. Many factors can assist agents in negotiating offers successfully.

The agent must allow for two important areas of preparation: a net sheet and an updated competitive market analysis. They serve critical roles in the decision-making process of the seller. The net sheet (see Figure 14-1, page 182) shows the seller, based on the offered price of the property, the approximate net dollars. The updated competitive market analysis shows the seller where the property is in the marketplace relative to comparable properties. This information furnishes the seller with information to consider before making an appropriate decision about an offer.

ARRANGING THE APPOINTMENT

Whenever an agent is put in the position of discussing an offer on the phone, he or she is at an extreme disadvantage. If one calls the sellers for an appointment to present an offer, it is almost certain that the seller will make inquiries about the offer. To avoid this it is best to have someone else in the office call the seller to schedule the appointment. This person simply calls the sellers and advises that the sellers' agent is going to be bringing a contract for their review and establishes a convenient time:

> *Ms. Jones, this is John Doe with ABC Realty. I'm calling on behalf of your agent, Jim Smith. Jim is unavailable at the moment and asked me to call you and find out if 7:30 this evening would be convenient for you and Mr. Jones to review a contract for the purchase of your home?*

If the time is not convenient, the agent should have alternative suggestions. The main concern is that the contract is presented as soon as possible to all parties whose approvals are necessary to consummate the sale.

PRESENTING THE OFFER TO THE SELLER

The most important aspect of dealing with the seller in the presentation of an offer is to anticipate what he or she will do. If one knows that the seller wants to reject any figure other than the listed price, one must be prepared to show the seller why he or she should consider a lesser amount (i.e., updated market analysis showing current comparable sales that may be lower than at the time of the listing).

It is best not to deal with anticipated problems until they arise, but one must be prepared for them. The agent should give a copy of the offer to each of the principals and review it with them. While the sellers are presented with a copy of the offer, they should be given the itemized sellers' net sheet showing what expenses are involved and how much they will net from the transaction. This must be prepared in advance, and the agent must be able to explain every item of the net sheet. Should there be an uneasiness obvious to the sellers during the presentation of the net sheet, it will be a negative factor that can cause them to doubt the accuracy of the figures. Therefore, thorough preparation is essential. Local assistance should be sought for detailed explanation of all items considered in calculating the seller's net dollars, as this will vary, depending upon the region of the country.

The Low Offer

When a written offer is presented to the agent, it must be submitted to the seller. Even though one often knows in advance the reaction of the seller, no agent has the right to decide what will and will not be brought to the attention of the seller. Therefore, the presentation of the low offer shouldn't be dreaded by the agent but rather looked upon as the fulfillment of a duty required by the code of ethics (if not by law) and a possible opportunity to obtain a counteroffer and reach some acceptable price for the property agreeable to both seller and buyer.

The best approach is to explain that it is a requirement that the agent present the offer.

> *Mr. and Ms. Seller, I am required to show you all offers that are received on your property. (With that slide a copy of the offer to the sellers and wait for their reactions.)*

Regardless of the reaction of the seller, the agent should never feel intimidated. The seller is reacting to the action of the buyer, not the agent. The agent must agree with the seller that the offer is too low and obtain a counteroffer.

> *Mr. and Ms. Seller, I am in complete agreement that this is not an offer that you should accept. This buyer obviously likes your home enough to go to the trouble of making an offer. What do you feel would be an acceptable price with which we could counter?*

Though it is sometimes difficult, one must get the sellers away from thinking about the low offer and to think about what they would accept.

Bringing the Seller Back to Reality

Frequently, sellers have a way of becoming somewhat out of touch with what they can really expect for their property even after a price has been established. Too often after an offer on the property, the sellers become inflexible regarding negotiation. Sometimes they will stand on principle over a very small difference between the listed price and the offered price. This is not always in their best interest. The agent must be prepared to deal with these lapses in reality.

First the agent must understand that few sellers feel that they really get what their property is worth. This needs to be accepted and dealt with in such a fashion as to inform the sellers that they are in fact receiving a very fair price for the property (when the agent feels that this is the case). In order to do this, the agent must show the sellers a completely updated market analysis showing the current values existing in today's marketplace. Secondly, one must bear in mind that completeness of information will play a major role in the acceptability of the advice that the agent wishes to convey. Everything should reflect thorough research and an accurate picture. In some instances, it might require the agent's showing the sellers other available properties priced comparably to the sellers'. In doing this, the sellers have an opportunity to see how the property fares in the marketplace. Sometimes nothing short of literally showing the sellers the properties in competition with their home will overcome the belief that their house is better than the rest.

'TOUCHY' SITUATIONS WITH SELLERS

Most "touchy" situations with sellers concern price. Every agent runs into the dilemma of needing to suggest that a seller accept a price lower than listed price and dealing with sellers' concern as to whether the agent is working for them or the buyers. For this reason, as well as the general sensitivity that most sellers have to money, such situations become "touchy."

The seller must consider various factors.

1. How long might the property remain on the market before another sale at a higher figure?

2. If the house is vacant, how much might it cost the seller while the property remains on the market in hopes of the higher sale?

3. For the transferee, isn't it better to have the house sold and have the family reunited than to wait for a higher sale?

4. In a situation where a seller doesn't need all of the proceeds from the sale of the house, isn't the sellers' carrying a note from the buyer secured by a second mortgage a good investment? If the buyer defaults, the sellers keep the buyer's money and get the house. They will get a good return on their money, have it secured by their own property, and get the best price for their home as well.

In such a situation, the agent must bring all considerations to the attention of the sellers in order to allow them to see exactly what their position is and what their options are.

GETTING THE OFFER ACCEPTED OR COUNTERED

Generally the sellers must consider that any decision resulting in no sale is like repurchasing the house. For instance, if the sellers are given an offer of $79,000 on their $80,000 house, they can accept the $79,000 offer and know that the house is sold, or they can counter at $80,000 and run the risk of losing the buyer, in which case they literally bought the house back for $80,000. This is important for the seller to realize. Additionally, the seller is gambling $79,000 to win $1,000. They have $79,000, and for that extra $1,000 they may lose it all.

No matter what happens when dealing with the sellers, the agent should never leave without a counteroffer, even one at full price. Negotiations must remain open. If a seller closes them by refusing to respond to a buyer's offer, he or she could well force the buyer to make an offer on another house, feeling that there is no future in negotiating on the home. While negotiations never cease unless the buyer refuses to make an additional offer, one must hope for the encouragement of the agent with whom the buyer is working. In such an instance, it would behoove the seller to counter rather than lose the buyer to another property.

One must also consider whether the buyer would have responded positively to a counteroffer by the seller and whether the seller would be pleased. Of course, the answer is *yes*. This must be explained to the seller. Buying homes is different from buying other items; the negotiations are played by different rules. Emotions play a great role in home purchases while they play minor roles in other transactions. For this reason, the seller should counter the offer in order to keep negotiations open. Once the offer has been rejected by the seller, and a failure to counter a buyer's offer can definitely be interpreted as a rejection by the seller, negotiations can be severed. Any kind of counteroffer is better than no counteroffer at all.

Frequently sellers will forget about the other things hinging on the sale of their properties and will deal with an offer without looking at it from the proper perspective. For this reason, it is wise for the agent to mention that should the sellers take the offer, the sellers would be able to proceed with a move to the country and can close on that new home that the sellers want so badly (or whatever the sellers' situation happens to be). Most importantly, the agent must show the sellers exactly what their position is in the marketplace (which is accomplished through the use of the updated competitive market analysis) and what proceeds they can expect from the sale of the property (through the use of a seller's net sheet).

PRESENTING THE COUNTEROFFER

As with scheduling an appointment to present an offer, the agent should have someone else set the appointment with the buyer to present the counteroffer. The important aspect of this approach is to avoid discussing the counteroffer on the telephone.

Bringing the Buyers Back to Reality

Frequently, buyers take the position with the agent that "if we don't get this one, we'll find another one." Certainly, there are lots of houses from which the buyer can choose, but the "right" house is hard to find. When the buyers find a house that they like well enough to make an offer on, they usually want the house. Their desire is usually strong enough to continue to negotiate with a reasonable seller.

Therefore, when a seller counters the buyer, the agent should reintroduce all the data offered to the buyer prior to the original offer (i.e., competitive market analysis). They should be reminded of the other properties shown and be reassured that the subject property is the best house for them. In some cases, it behooves the agent to reshow the buyer the subject property and another house or two to strengthen the buyer's conviction. The agent must, however, avoid showing the buyer homes not yet seen if at all possible. Often new properties will only confuse the buyer and cause second thoughts about the house that he or she really wants.

Reselling the Buyers

Utilizing the market analysis is effective with the buyers not only when making the offer but also when considering a counteroffer. It shows the buyers the value of houses in the area, houses that are not nearly as close to satisfying the buyers' needs as the house on which they have made an offer. The conveniences that a home offers are the reasons that it is special and why one should consider offering an amount that will ensure the purchase.

Getting the Counteroffer Accepted

When the agent knows how much the buyers want the house on which they've made an offer, the agent should stress the things making this house special to the buyers. Reiterating the strong points of the house and making verbal comparisons to other houses that the buyers have seen is important. A reference to the buyers' timetable and any other factors that the buyers must consider is wise on the agent's part. It is best to deal with the amount of difference between the originally offered price and the countered price, rather than the countered price itself. In this way the buyers will consider the sellers' counter in the proper perspective. Many times the difference between the two (offered price and countered price) is so small that it is not worth agonizing over.

When enormous differences are involved, the buyers must refer to the competitive market analysis to see exactly how the house is priced in relation to the marketplace. The analysis will prove extremely effective when prepared and used properly. On some occasions, the agent will again be forced to reshow the buyers some of the houses that led to this decision. This can be dangerous as it consumes much time, and the house that the buyers want may be sold in the interim.

The Ping Pong Syndrome

Every attempt should be made by the agent to avoid a situation whereby the buyer and seller are continually splitting the difference. This will result in an unceasing ping pong between the two. If it arises where one of the parties (buyer or seller) wishes to split the difference, the agent should attempt to have one of them offer an amount not equivalent to 50 percent of the outstanding difference. This avoids establishing a precedent in terms of the amount of compromise that either party will make.

Proper Perspective

One must remember to keep negotiations in their proper perspective. Individuals involved in negotiations can often become emotional and allow their emotions to cause them to do things not in their best interest. A typical example occurs when a buyer makes an offer considered unreasonably low by the seller. As a result, the seller may choose to reject the offer entirely and write on the offer that he or she will not negotiate on the sale of the property with the buyer. Of course, the listing agreement provides that the buyer can continue to offer on the property, but the seller will be difficult to deal with and the buyer can easily become discouraged.

This situation occurs because the seller has allowed himself or herself to lose perspective. The agent must attempt to show the seller that this buyer may prove to be the one who pays a price acceptable to the seller and therefore he or she should continue to negotiate with him or her and counter the offer. This is when the agent really earns the fee and often represents the only positive force holding the transaction together.

COMMUNICATING ACCEPTANCE OF THE OFFER

Once acceptance has been obtained, the party waiting for the response of the other should be told with great enthusiasm. Obviously, whoever last counters the contract hopes to have the proposal accepted by the other party. He or she is expressing what is acceptable to him or her and must wait for approval or rejection. There is a certain amount of stress in such a situation. When one is successful, it is followed by a tremendous feeling of relief. The degree to which this relief is experienced is somewhat dependent upon how the agent conveys this information.

Some choose to take a low-keyed, this-is-just-an-everyday-kind-of-thing attitude when communicating final acceptance. This misses a great opportunity to heighten the pleasure from the victory of having a request accepted. Since this request is expressed by the individual making the offer or counteroffer, its acceptance is one that is awaited with some degree of anticipation. For this reason, a message such as "Congratulations," "I've got great news," "We did it," etc., should be part of the way one informs the buyer or seller of an accepted offer.

(*Note:* To avoid any legal ramifications surrounding the processing of counteroffers, the agent should consult an attorney for current court rulings regarding the extent of obligations by either party when making a counteroffer.)

Exercise

List all the preparation that should take place before one attempts to present an offer or counteroffer.

17

Goal Setting

Much has been written regarding this most necessary ingredient for success, yet it remains one of the most loosely practiced principles within our society. Why so few people practice goal setting in its true form is difficult to say. Most people who have been exposed to goal setting in one form or another rarely take it seriously. In all probability, it is because goal setting is easy to avoid. All one needs to do is to establish an amount of money that one wishes to earn, and he or she has set a goal.

Goal setting is much more than this if it is to be effective. It is difficult for most people to do because they have so little, if any, frame of reference on the subject. Were their parents involved in goal setting? Probably they were not. The individual finds reasons for not doing it rather than reasons for doing it. Not being exposed to goal setting while growing up or attending school keeps many people swimming in waters of mediocrity.

People frequently, in an attempt to justify why they don't need to set goals, cite examples of people who have succeeded without setting goals. In reply, one could ask what they would have achieved with goals. The life insurance industry conducted a study to determine the extent to which people progress in life. They took 100 men at age 25 and actually tracked their progress for 40 years. Each of these individuals was the same age. None had any educational or financial edge over the others. By age 65, 36 had died. Of the remaining 64 men, only 1 was wealthy, 4 were financially independent, 5 still had to work, and 54 were financially insolvent. These surprising results can undoubtedly be attributed, at least in part, to poorly defined goals. The realization that over half the people who pursue a career are literally broke after 40 years is staggering.

We all tend to identify with what we're used to. Most people tend to reject something new or different or that they don't understand. The first thing that must be done to hope to achieve one's potential is to realize how the world is. What was fine for another generation is not necessarily fine today. Unfortunately, the way things ought to be (our frame of reference) and the way things are (reality) can be quite different. It was best expressed in Susan Howatch's book *Sins of the Fathers*. A character in the book who was tremendously successful told his four young proteges, "You must deal with the way things *really are*, not the way they *ought to be*."

OBJECTIVES OF GOAL SETTING

There are three main objectives in setting goals:

1. **Establish Direction.** Failure stems from a lack of direction. Knowing what and where we are and what we are setting out to achieve, is essential. Though one can have some overall understanding of this, it is never as apparent as when one sets clearly defined goals.

2. **Maximize Productivity.** Everyone extends energy throughout the day, frequently with poor results. A person knows that he or she could and should do much more than actually is done. Goals are a means of harnessing one's energy and thereby maximizing productivity.

3. **Attain Potential.** Nothing in life can be regarded as a greater achievement than attaining one's potential. To be the best one can is all that one can ask of oneself. Goal setting is the most important step in the chain of events leading to this greatest of all accomplishments.

WHAT DOES IT ACHIEVE?

Goal setting helps achieve three of the most crucial requirements for success:

1. **A Sense of Direction and Purpose.** One cannot truly maintain one's tenacity unless one has identified direction and purpose. Goals bring this to the forefront.

2. **Motivation.** Unless one is highly motivated, one cannot expect to achieve great things. Motivation is nothing more than one's level of enthusiasm. Anyone who has ever worked at achieving anything knows only too well that if there is no enthusiasm for the project, one will not only lose interest but will not approach the project with a great deal of optimism. Motivation from within is essential and goals help to nurture motivation. As one sees one's goal becoming more and more a reality, the enthusiasm for what is necessary to make that goal an achievement is inevitable.

3. **Self-Discipline.** Most people have great trouble in maintaining a high degree of self-discipline and usually fall far short of what is necessary to accomplish success. However, with goals, self-discipline becomes an accepted and practiced quality of even the most undisciplined.

WHAT HAPPENS WITHOUT GOALS?

The lack of goals can bring about disastrous results. Generally we find that when one fails to plan goals, he or she becomes satisfied, neglects the basics, becomes lazy, utilizes time poorly, and ends up in a slump. This is only natural since most of these problems occur in the lives of people who have no sense of direction or purpose, lack motivation, and have little, if any, self-discipline.

Naturally, there are exceptions, as there are to everything in life. The question is, Is it worth the chance of experiencing all these problems, when they can be largely avoided through goal setting?

SETTING REALISTIC FINANCIAL GOALS

The REALTOR®s National Marketing Institute has reported on a goal study by Harvard University regarding alumni 20 years after graduation. They found that 83 percent of those surveyed had no specific goals at all. Fourteen percent had specific goals and were earning 3 times as much as those with no specific goals. The remaining 3 percent not only had specific goals but had them in writing and were earning 10 times as much as the group with no specific goals (3⅓ times as much as those with goals not in writing).

In order to maximize the benefits of goal setting, goals must be in writing. To do this effectively, one must sit down with paper and pencil and do some serious soul searching to determine what to set one's sights on and commit oneself to pursue. It is first necessary to determine what one must have, that is, reduce to writing all expenses incurred in order to maintain one's life style. That is, specifically, what the income must be in the next year.

Example

Expense	Monthly	Annually
Mortgage payment	$400	$4,800
Car payments	300	3,600
Furniture payment	75	900
Groceries	200	2,400
Child care	150	1,800
Clothing	100	1,200
Physician and prescriptions	100	1,200
Entertainment	100	1,200
Incidentals	100	1,200
Totals	$1,525	$18,300

These figures do not include any local, state, or federal taxes, which will influence these totals in terms of actual net dollars. One must allow for such taxes in order to get a clear and accurate picture of amounts necessary.

At this point one can see that unless one earns $18,300 in the coming 12 months ($1,525 per month), it will be impossible to meet these obligations. Most people seem to earn what must be earned. The purpose of financial goal setting is not merely to meet one's obligations but rather to increase them. Therefore, having established what one must have, the next step is to look into increasing it.

CREATING NEEDS

Almost everyone has a figure in mind as to what he or she would like in terms of earnings, an amount that would allow the individual to breathe a bit easier and get ahead. We will concern ourselves with this since one must first get into the habit of goal setting and make it work before one can reasonably expect to tackle large, long-range earning goals.

Let's use the example of $44,000 as an annual earning goal. If one felt that this would serve as a genuinely reasonable amount of money for a year's work and would be pleased with it, it must be compared to what one must have.

Earning goal	$44,000
Less current budget	− 18,300
Earning difference	$25,700

Now the question is, What shall become of this $25,700? Planning on putting it into a savings account is not enough. We established earlier that one tends to earn what one must have; if one stops here, the likelihood is that $18,300 is all that will be earned. Therefore, needs must be created for the balance:

Family vacation	$ 3,000
Investment in rental property	10,000
Summer camp for children	2,000
New furniture for dining room	3,500
Remodeled playroom	4,000
Children's college fund	3,000
Wedding anniversary dinner	200
Total	$25,700*

*One must allow for all taxes which will affect this amount.

At this point, the $25,700 is no longer merely a figure. It represents a vacation, an investment, camp for the children, new furniture, money toward the children's education, and a great evening for a wedding anniversary. Additional needs are apparent for which the additional earnings will be used.

What we have done is no different than what any well-run company does. We've projected profits and earmarked them for future use. We have begun to act like serious business people.

In addition to the agent's planning these goals, he or she must include those people affected by these earnings. If, for instance, one's spouse does not work and is dependent upon the agent for the future, the agent must include the spouse in the establishment of these goals. Not only is it selfish to exclude the spouse from this, but it will cause the agent to fall short of real needs. Goal setting must be a joint effort by all affected parties.

STRUCTURING THE PLAN

The previous example of $44,000 must be converted into the activities that will result in these earnings. What is necessary in order to earn $44,000? One must first determine what activities will produce this earning goal. If the primary sources of earnings come from listing and selling, what percentage of this goal will be derived from each? Exactly what activities are necessary to produce a sale and a sold listing? How many times a month should one be involved in these activities? All these questions must be answered before one can effectively develop a plan of action to achieve one's goal.

For our example, I am going to make some ratios and estimates (these are only for the purposes of example; the agent must determine what is true to him or her and his or her company):

Percentage of income from listing	50%
Percentage of income from selling	50%
Average listing commission per transaction	$1,000
Average selling commission per transaction	$1,000
Number of months agent will work this year (net)	11
Percentage of listing presentations that result in listings	33⅓%
Percentage of listings that sell	50%
Percentage of potential sellers who grant an appointment	50%
Percentage of customers who are sold	33⅓%
Percentage of customers contacted who work with agent	50%

The preceding is necessary in order to plan adequately what one must do to attain one's goal. With this information, we can determine the correct plan for attaining the goal of $44,000 using the goal sheet (Figure 17-1). The form is most beneficial because it breaks down earnings into the most simple form of effort that ultimately results in the production level which produces the desired income.

Annual earning goal $ __44,000__

__50%__ of income from listings sold $ __22,000__

__50%__ of income from sales made $ __22,000__

$ __22,000__ listing commission @$ __1,000__ per listing sold requires __22__ listings sold.

Based on __11__ months in a work year requires __2__ listings sold per month. __2__ listings must be taken in order to result in __1__ listings sold. So __4__ listings must be taken per month.

__3__ listing appointments to obtain one listing. This shall require __12__ listing appointments per month.

__2__ listing appointment attempts to obtain one listing appointment. This will require __24__ listing appointment attempts each month for the balance of year.

In order to produce $ __22,000__ income from sales @$ __1,000__ per sale, you will need to make __22__ sales this year. This will require __2__ sales per month.

If you sell __33⅓%__ of the customers you show, this will require you to show __6__ buyers per month. If you show __50%__ of the customers you attempt to show, you need __12__ showing appointment attempts per month.

Conclusion:

__24__ listing appointment attempts = __12__ listing appointments = __4__ listings = __2__ listings sold @ $ __1,000__ per listing sold = $ __2,000__ per month.

__12__ showing appointment attempts = __6__ showing appointments = __2__ sales @ $ __1,000__ per sale = $ __2,000__ per month.

Total monthly listing income	= $	2,000
Total monthly sales income	= $	2,000
Total monthly income	= $	4,000
Number of months	=	× 11
Total annual earnings	= $	44,000

Figure 17-1. Goal Sheet

In the example, one can see that 24 listing appointment attempts should result in 12 listing appointments, which should result in 4 listings, which should produce 2 listings sold. (These calculations are based on the arbitrary ratios chosen for use in this example. Each agent and company must substitute applicable ratios.) The listings sold are worth $1,000 each, for a total listing income of $2,000 per month. Then, 12 showing appointment attempts should result in showing houses to 6 different buyers, which should result in 2 sales. Each sale is worth $1,000 per sale, for a total sales income of $2,000 per month.

Based on this information, one can easily recognize that unless continuous and consistent attempts are made each month to produce the desired numbers of appointments, sales and listings will not occur. Unless attempts to secure these appointments are initiated, everything else becomes academic. This process allows the agent to view the pursuit of goals from the proper perspective.

PROGRESS MEASUREMENT AND GOAL REVISION

After the goal has been set and the plan has been formulated by using the goal sheet, one must frequently refer to the goal sheet to measure progress. The agent may be working in exact accordance with the goals; in other cases he or she may run ahead or behind of what has been set.

If one is running behind, there must be a change. That change can well be goal revision. One may find that the ratios established are no longer accurate in view of a change in the marketplace. In some cases one may find that it is necessary to make more calls, presentations, and showings to result in the desired number of listings and sales necessary to achieve the goal. Only through these revisions and changes can one maintain one's goals.

WHAT TO REMEMBER ABOUT GOALS

We have been talking about annual earning goals. Obviously, one must think beyond next year and about where one would like to be in three, four, and five years. These long-range goals become the whole essence of why one works. The short-range goal tells one how to work, and that is important. The long-range goals will take one's life in the direction that it travels. An agent's long-range goals will depend on what he or she wants from life. Though it is important to be realistic in what to achieve in a short timeframe, such as a year, the agent should never feel that long-range goals are unrealistic. There are are no unrealistic goals, only unrealistic timetables. The problem occurs when one doesn't allow adequate time to attain goals. Consequently, people are discouraged and give up when success is just around the corner. No plane can take off unless the runway is long enough; life is the same way.

Many years ago the Texas multimillionaire, H. L. Hunt, was interviewed and asked for the secret to success. He replied in his homespun manner that "you got to know what it is you want, want it with all your heart, expect to get it, and decide what you are willing to give up for it."

This message gives us the four essentials for ultimate success:

1. Know exactly what you want—have a clearly defined goal.
2. Want it with everything in you—be committed to the goal.
3. Confidently expect to attain the goal—believe in yourself.
4. Be prepared to sacrifice in order to attain it—you must sacrifice in order to achieve.

PERSONAL GOALS BEYOND EARNINGS

We have discussed earning goals and have not talked about the other things in life, which are just as important, if no more so, than money. We are all working for many reasons, one of which is definitely to achieve some kind of financial security. However, in the course of goal setting we must include other things important to us, such as family, health, education, religion, the community, etc. For a well-balanced life, all areas must be provided for.

Exercise

Using the figures and ratios in the example within this chapter, work a goal sheet, using an annual earning goal of $33,000.

18

Time Management
and Selling Real Estate

People who know me commonly refer to the following as *Sam's Law:* Never, ever, ever do anything that you can get someone else to do for you. Due to the impossibility of accomplishing as much independently as one can through the efforts of others, one should delegate all that one can. Certain problems accompany the utilization of time. The biggest problem with improving one's ability to manage time is that most people feel that they utilize their time well. Certainly, there is some room for improvement, but overall they feel that they do adequately.

This is a problem because unless one recognizes inefficiency, one rarely does much to improve. If one approaches time management with an attitude that it is a science and a great concern, then one will get the most from one's time. If, however, a person desires to look for a tip or two since he or she is already doing a grand job, the person will gain only that, a tip or two.

OBJECTIVES

Depending on one's particular goals in life, any number of objectives can be identified and benefits derived from effective time management. Obviously, some important ones are:

1. More accomplishments in less time
2. Greater control over one's life

215

3. Increased earnings
4. Time to initiate new ideas
5. Time to develop new programs
6. More time for one's family
7. More time for oneself
8. Ability to enjoy oneself and not feel guilty about being away from the office

REALITY AND TIME MANAGEMENT

Any number of excuses can be used for not implementing a program to utilize time more effectively. This is not facing reality. No matter how busy one is, one must take time to plan. While this is not always the most desirable event in the day due to hectic schedules, schedules are usually hectic because of poor time utilization.

Additionally, the less time one has for such things, the more important it is to plan activities. As with goal setting (Chapter 17), what one has been able to do without effective time management is nowhere near what could be done with it.

GETTING CONTROL

In the quest of control of one's time, one must examine the available choices. How productive one's time will become is in direct relationship to the choices made in how one spends time. Making these choices accurately regarding how one uses time is more critical than doing a task efficiently. One must ask, how productive are the things that I do? In most cases, the average agent is more concerned with the quality of the work, rather than with the productivity or value of the task. Of course, one must be efficient and always strive to do well and with great efficiency. Before taking on a task one must weigh its significance within the available options. As Alan Lakein notes in his book, *How to Get Control of Your Time and Your Life*, "It is not worthwhile to make a big effort for a task of little value." Does one know how to assess the value of one's efforts? More importantly, does one assess the value of available choices?

In an effort to control his or her time, an agent must determine all options and assess the value of each in order to make the correct decisions. This can only be done effectively by making a list of the options and assessing the value of each. One can easily prioritize activities and act according to the priority of the task.

The agent should begin by making a list of available activities during a workday. If this isn't done, many things are forgotten. The following action list is an example of what an agent *could* do in the course of a normal work day. (For this example, we are using only work-related tasks and no personal responsibilities [i.e., family activities, social functions, etc.]. These areas of one's life have been omitted due to the varying priorities that readers would place on them, not in any way to minimize their importance.)

Action List

Update listing files

Schedule appointments with sellers and other companies to show their houses

Qualify buyers

Prepare for a listing presentation

Prepare a competitive market analysis

Write ads

Put up for-sale signs

Preview houses

Attend a closing

Deliver papers to the closer's office

Check tax records

Meet appraisers

Check with lenders for current interest rates

Follow up on pending transactions

Prepare for an open house

Show houses

Service listings

Attend meetings and educational programs

FSBO preparation

Call FSBOs

Write and negotiate offers

Schedule inspections

Make an action list

Take down signs

Pay bills and do personal bookkeeping

Check newspaper for ads on properties that agent has been unable to locate for a buyer

Prospecting

Opportunity time (property time)

Return phone calls

Correspondence and paperwork

Listing appointments

Hold open house

While this list does not represent all that one could do, let's examine it. One can see that it would be impossible for anyone to accomplish all these tasks in a normal workday. This alone gives credence to the necessity of prioritizing tasks so that what one spends time doing is in fact the most valuable task. Each task could, under the right set of circumstances, become more important than ordinarily. Barring such a situation, we should view each area of the agent's work life with a value on each task that *ordinarily* is correct.

MAXIMIZING RESULTS OF THE TIME EXPENDED

Lakein addresses the necessity of time prioritization in what he calls the *ABC's* of time management, which he defines as follows:

- A's — high-value items (things that must be done to-day, i.e., show houses to a buyer; attend a closing)
- B's — medium-value items (things that should be done today but not at the expense of an A, i.e., deliver material to the neighborhood that agent specializes within)
- C's — low-value items (things that if never done, nothing is lost, i.e., fill out political questionnaire)

Additionally, these A's, B's, and C's must be divided into subgroups, such as A_1, A_2, A_3, A_4; B_1, B_2, B_3, B_4; C_1, C_2, C_3, C_4. In doing this, one can arrive at the exact order of importance of each of the tasks.

   While there will always be a difference of opinion when prioritizing tasks, let's examine our list after it has been prioritized.

Action List

B_{11} Update listing files

A_6 Schedule appointments with sellers and other companies to show their houses

A_{10} Qualify a buyer

A_3 Prepare for a listing presentation

A_4 Prepare a competitive market analysis

B_9 Write ads

B_3 Put up for-sale signs

B_6 Preview houses

A_9 Attend a closing

A_8 Deliver papers to the closer's office

B_{12} Check tax records

B_4 Meet appraisers

B_{10} Check with lenders for current interest rates

A_{17} Follow up on pending transactions

A_{15} Prepare for an open house

A_7 Show houses

B_5 Service listings

A_{11} Attend meetings and educational programs

A_{12} FSBO preparation

A_{13} Call FSBOs

A_2 Write and negotiate offers

B_2 Schedule inspections

A_1 Make an action list

C Take down signs

B_{13} Pay bills and do personal bookkeeping

B_1 Check newspaper for ads on properties that agent has been unable to locate for a buyer

A_{14} Prospecting

A_{18} Opportunity time (proper-
ty time)
B_7 Return phone calls

B_8 Correspondence and paperwork
A_5 Listing appointments
A_{16}Hold open house

One can readily see that by prioritizing this list of 32 tasks, we have identified 18 high-value items (items such as A_3 and A_4 are necessary in order to perform A_5; therefore, the list of A's must include those tasks allowing one to be prepared adequately for the main function, which produces a result), 13 medium-value items, and 1 low-value item. By concentrating on the high-value items, one can bring about the maximum amount of productivity in the shortest amount of time.

This is merely the tip of the iceberg. While concentrating on high-value items increases productivity, to be most effective the agent must delegate as much work as possible in order to spend time only on the specific tasks that, when successful, produce some form of valuable activity (i.e., listing, sale, potential customers).

An example of the benefits from delegating for maximum effectiveness, would be A_3, A_4, and A_5. Preparing for the listing interview (A_3) and preparing the competitive market analysis (A_4) were high-value items because they had to take place in order to make the listing appointment (A_5) successful. However, both the preparation for the listing interview and the preparation of a competitive market analysis could be delegated.

Whether the agent has someone to whom this work can be delegated is unimportant. The main issue is that if such a person existed, this could be turned over to him or her, thus freeing the agent for other things. If one can agree that this would be a more efficient way to operate, then he or she must make further considerations. Certainly, if someone else could do such time-consuming tasks, perhaps other tasks could also be performed by others. If the total of this delegated time is significant, it merits the agent's hiring someone to assist in the work.

Let's examine how many of these tasks could be delegated to another, if one had an assistant working to lighten the workload. Such items are crossed out on the following list.

Action List

B_{11} ~~Update listing files~~
A_6 ~~Schedule appointments with sellers and other companies to show their houses~~

A_{10} Qualify a buyer
A_3 ~~Prepare for a listing presentation~~
A_4 ~~Prepare a competitive market analysis~~

~~B₉ Write ads~~
~~B₃ Put up for-sale signs~~
B₆ Preview houses
A₉ Attend a closing
~~A₈ Deliver papers to the clos-
er's office~~
~~B₁₂ Check tax records~~
~~B₄ Meet appraisers~~
~~B₁₀ Check with lenders for
current interest rates~~
~~A₁₇ Follow-up on pending
transactions~~
~~A₁₅ Prepare for an open house~~
A₇ Show houses
B₅ Service listings
A₁₁ Attend meetings and edu-
cational programs
~~A₁₂ FSBO preparation~~
A₁₃ Call FSBOs

A₂ Write and negotiate offers
~~B₂ Schedule inspections~~
A₁ Make an action list
~~C Take down signs~~
~~B₁₃ Pay bills and do personal
bookkeeping~~
~~B₁ Check newspaper for ads
on properties that agent
has been unable to locate
for a buyer~~
A₁₄ Prospecting
A₁₈ Opportunity time (proper
ty time)
~~B₇ Return phone calls~~
~~B₈ Correspondence and paper
work~~
A₅ Listing appointments
A₁₆ Hold open house

The following items remain on the agent's list:

Action List

A₁ Make an Action List
A₂ Write and negotiate offers
A₃ Listing appointments
A₄ Show houses
A₅ Attend a closing
A₆ Qualify a buyer
A₇ Attend meetings and edu-
cational programs

A₈ Call FSBO's
A₉ Prospecting
A₁₀ Hold open house
A₁₁ Opportunity time (proper-
ty time)
B₁ Service Listings
B₂ Preview houses

Immediately, one can reduce this list of 32 tasks to 13 tasks and delegate 19 to an assistant. This is a reduction of one's workload by almost 60 percent. We have eliminated all low-value tasks, eleven medium-value tasks, and seven high-value tasks, thus leaving the more manageable number of 13 tasks. By delegating to improve effectiveness, the agent will have more time to spend on *high-value tasks.*

Where does one get this assistant? It is economically impossible for any company to provide each agent with an assistant. While there may be a secretary in the office to help the agents with their work, this is not to mean that any one agent can monopolize the time of the secretary. He or she is there for everyone. If there were an even distribution of the secretary's time, in an 8-hour workday, within a 10-agent office, each agent would get the secretary for a whopping 48 minutes. This is hardly practical for truly delegating.

For this reason, each agent should strongly consider positioning himself or herself so that at some point he or she can hire an assistant. This may be unconventional, but the facts clearly show how important such an individual is to the career advancement of a real estate agent. There is no way of handling a large amount of business without an assistant (not to mention additionally finding time for one's family and outside interests). An assistant will prove worth far more than what he or she is paid. Such a person can easily provide the agent with an additional 50 or 60 hours a per month.

The utilization of such an individual will not only allow the agent to handle much more business but will forever change the agent's life. Having an individual to take most of the unproductive tasks off the shoulders of the agent will be an arrangement which the agent must never be without again. One's potential will never truly be attainable without someone to assist.

MAXIMIZING THE ASSISTANT'S INVOLVEMENT

Whenever the discussion of hiring an assistant comes up among most agents, there are many pessimistic comments about how much such a person can actually do. No one licensed to sell real estate has learned anything that others cannot. Agents who have traditionally performed those low-value tasks and felt that "this is what the seller is hiring me for" (i.e., their ability to prepare a competitive market analysis, write effective ads, etc.) are sadly mistaken. Most tasks performed by agents could be performed by someone else if this individual were trained to perform these tasks. This is the real secret of maximizing the results of an assistant: train well. One must first list tasks to be delegated to the assistant in the form of a job description. This job description should state exactly what the assistant will do and how. It is then the agent's responsibility to find an individual who is responsible enough to perform these tasks and then train this person to perform these tasks to the agent's satisfaction.

Only the agent can identify what should be included in the assistant's job description. The agent should progress in stages and slowly delegate more and more to the individual, until the agent is able to turn over everything he or she wishes which does not require a real estate license to perform. In referring to the action list of 32 tasks, one could, with a minimal amount of explanation, immediately turn over the following to an assistant:

1. Schedule appointments with sellers and other companies to show their houses
2. Put up for-sale signs
3. Deliver papers to the closer's office
4. Check with lenders for current interest rates
5. Prepare for an open house
6. Prepare for FSBO (cutting out FSBO ads and cross-referencing the phone numbers for the name and address of the advertiser)
7. Schedule mechanical and termite inspections
8. Put up sold signs
9. Take down signs
10. Do correspondence

Using this as a starting point, the agent can gradually delegate more and more work to the assistant. As one delegates more detail work, such as writing ads, preparing a competitive market analysis, etc., the agent must spend additional time with the assistant for training in the best way to go about accomplishing the task and the manner in which the agent wants it done.

In some cases the assistant is better at some of these tasks than the agent. Writing ads is often a task for which the agent can use all the help he or she can get. After the assistant previews the property, he or she is often able to write a better and more effective ad than the agent. This can also be true of time-consuming detail work, such as a competitive market analysis. Many agents are not good at detail work while an assistant may. Often the assistant prepares not only a more detailed competitive market analysis but a more effective one as well. The agent's time is too valuable to spend doing things that someone else could do.

KEEPING TIME WORKING

In order to get the most from effective time management, the agent must have alternative plans for every occasion. For instance, when an agent has scheduled a showing appointment with a buyer at 9:30

a.m. and has allotted 3 hours for this buyer, the agent must have an alternative plan if the buyer cancels. Failing to create these alternative plans is to fail to utilize one's time effectively. Sooner or later every agent has a buyer or potential seller cancel an appointment. Just knowing that something else should be done in such instances is not enough. The agent must know what he or she would do.

Many alternative plans can be held in reserve; basically they are other items on the action list. Calling for-sale-by-owners can be done at any time and is always good to do when appointments cancel. While one would prefer to do *A* tasks, in some cases it may be just the time to get rid of some of the *B*'s, such as return phone calls, service listings, etc.

Another important aspect of effective time management is the area that Lakein calls *external prime time*. This is defined as the best time to work with others. If asked the question, what is the overall best time of the day to get together with both husband and wife, be they buyers or sellers?, surely the answer would be in the evening. Since the greatest numbers of people are available in the evenings, real estate agents should identify this as their external prime time. Each agent must schedule himself or herself in the office a certain number of evenings every week. Working in the evenings when a customer merits it is not the point (i.e., showing houses to one who wishes to look at houses today at 6:30 p.m.). This is merely taking care of what circumstances have dictated. Rather, this activity requires initiating an effort not requested by a buyer or seller. For instance, an agent decides that every Monday, Wednesday, and Thursday evening from 7:00 until 10:00 p.m. he or she will be at the office, calling those individuals whom he or she was unable to locate during the day. This is properly taking advantage of external prime time. Unfortunately, most agents feel that they will do these things from their homes; with all the interruptions at home they do little.

Exercise

1. Identify 50 tasks that the agent could do, both business and personal, and rate how you feel about them, using the *ABC* method.

2. Eliminate from the list all those items that could be delegated to another, moving up in number those remaining.

19

Do It Now!

The following advice from George Bernard Shaw is especially appropriate to a career in real estate sales:

You must take care to get what you like or you will be forced to like what you get.

As a real estate agent, either you take the steps necessary to achieve success or you spend the rest of your life trying to justify whatever happens—or fails to happen. Many people make excuses for lack of productivity, putting the blame on market conditions (interest rates, time of the year, and so on), but the fact is, an agent makes his or her *own* market. Overall market conditions never keep top agents from producing—that's why they *are* top agents.

One of the most exciting things about the real estate business is that it enables you to control your own destiny. This industry exemplifies the very meaning of the American dream—not asking for a handout or charity, but only for opportunity. And in real estate, opportunities are always there, regardless of market conditions. People always buy and sell homes, and taking advantage of opportunities to obtain a share of that business is what free enterprise is all about. Under no circumstances must a real estate agent succumb to so-called "inconquerable limitations." As long as one thinks, analyzes, plans, and acts, success is inevitable. It may take time, but it is inevitable.

THE AGENT AS PARTNER

An agent is a partner in all real estate. The real estate license grants the privilege of receiving a commission from the sale of any real estate in the licensing state, provided the agent is involved in the transaction and a commission is being paid. The right is uniquely the agent's by virtue of that license.

In order to understand the extent of this partnership, one must first determine how the commission that is received translates. As an example,* if an agent lists and sells a $100,000 property and receives $3,000 as his or her share of the commission, is this not the equivalent of an indirect 3 percent ownership of the property? To take the example a step further, if the seller's equity in the $100,000 property were $30,000, is the agent's $3,000 not equivalent to an indirect 10 percent equity position in the property? This is what every agent has the right to claim in presenting the only acceptable form of "proof of ownership"—creativity. If an agent can only be creative enough to find the need on the part of an owner to sell, and a need on the part of an individual to invest, he or she cashes in that percentage.

DARE TO BE DIFFERENT

What makes top producers different from other agents? This question has been asked many times. On the surface, there is no basic difference among agents. Most possess the same ability to perceive and produce, the same capacity for work, the same desire for the rewards of success, the same potential. The only identifiable difference is not found in the overabundance of any quality or trait, save one: top producers will do what others will not do or are afraid to do.

A willingness to do things differently and a desire to make a better tomorrow for oneself and one's family are found within every successful person. Doing things the way others do them is not always the best way; refusing to accept things as they are is expressing a desire to grow. Most people tend to resist or reject what is different or what they do not understand. Successful people are always searching for a better way to do things and are never afraid to question anything that they do not understand.

---

*This is purely for the purpose of an example and is in no way to be construed as typical or recommended.

To question, to seek to understand, to think, and then to decide is to refuse to be simply one of the masses. Mediocrity comes at us from every direction. There is always safety in numbers, even if it is only safety from being criticized for being different. In the final analysis, however, throughout history the people we most admire and revere are those who were not afraid to look over the next hill, to question what most others believed to be true. Without people who dared to be different, who refused to accept a life of complacency and stood by their convictions, who, as Thoreau wrote, "stepped to the beat of a different drummer," there would have been no discoveries, no inventions . . . no change.

THE FUTURE IS NOW

Yesterday is dead and gone—nothing can ever bring it back or change it. Tomorrow is yet to be experienced; what it will hold is unknown, but it will very definitely reflect what you do today. In reality, it is what you do today that governs your life. Your future begins now. Your career must be changed now. Everything you want in your life must be planned and pursued today—not tomorrow, but *today*. Today is the most important time of your life. Treat it as such.

Epilogue

Good luck in your real estate career! I have attempted to share as many different aspects of successful approaches to listing and selling real estate as possible. Now it's up to you.

Since this has been a one-way conversation, if you have any comments, questions, opinions or would like to write me for any reason, you may do so in care of the Real Estate Editor, Reston Publishing Co., 11480 Sunset Hills Road, Reston, Virginia 22090.

Glossary

Area of Geographical Specialization. A specific area within which an agent chooses to specialize.

Advertising Specialty Companies. Companies which supply items imprinted with agent's and company's name for use as give-aways.

Brainstorming. A method of using various ideas stemming from a given assignment for the purpose of producing the best and most complete ideas regarding the assignment. This can be done by one or more people and is effectively done when using guides for thought stimulation such as listing ideas by letters of the alphabet, then eliminating those not applicable and building on those proving valuable.

Centers of Influence. People that the agent knows who are in a position to send the agent business or assist the agent in obtaining business.

Client. The individual who has contracted with the agent for his or her services and has agreed to pay a fee for said services. Though this is traditionally the seller, it can also be the buyer if such contractual agreement is executed between buyer and agent (i.e., buyer agrees to pay agent a commission on the purchase price of property if agent is successful in finding such property for buyer).

Close. The initiative by the salesperson which, when acknowledged, will verify that the customer or client is in agreement.

Closing Question. A question asked by the salesperson to the customer or client, the answer to which confirms purchase of the item or service being presented.

Commission. The remuneration that the agent receives for successfully consummating a transaction, in the form of a percentage of the sale price.

Commission Rate. The rate of percentage of the sale price which makes up the commission.

Commission Schedule. The manner in which the real estate company and real estate agent associated with that company divide the total commission.

Comparables. Similar properties used to determine the value of the property in question.

Competitive Market Analysis. A form which illustrates the comparables on a piece of property for the purpose of showing the client or customer how a piece of property compares to others of its type which are for sale, which did not sell, and which were sold.

Cooperating Commission Split. The arrangement which real estate companies follow in the division of commission when they are involved in the same transaction (i.e., the property is listed by one company and sold by another).

Counteroffer. The altering of an offer to purchase indicating that the previous offer was unacceptable and showing the amount and terms that are acceptable.

Cross Reference Directory. A directory from which one can determine the resident of a property and published phone number by locating the address, and the name and address of an individual by locating the phone number.

Customer. The person or persons who seek the assistance of the agent but who do not pay the agent's fee.

Disqualifying Question. Questions asked by buyers over the phone which, when answered, either eliminate the property or terminate the conversation.

Door-to-Door Public Relations. A method of creating continuity within a geographical area for the purpose of becoming the dominant listing agent in that area.

Earnest Money. Money deposited in good faith by the purchaser at the time of making an offer on a property.

Estimated Closing Statement. A form which shows the buyer the total estimated cost of acquiring a property, and the seller the estimated net dollars that he or she will receive from the sale of the property. Also known as 'Net Sheet.'

Exclusive Listing. The type of listing which is used by real estate agents. The term exclusive listing is frequently used within real estate circles for the Exclusive Right to Sell.

Exclusive Right to Sell. A listing agreement between seller and agent granting to said agent the irrevocable right to offer the property for sale at a given price and terms for a given period of time. If the property is sold within the stated period of time agent shall receive the remuneration provided for in the contract regardless of whether the property sells by agent, other real estate agent, or seller.

Farming. See *Door-To-Door Public Relations.*

Floor Time. That designated time of the day during which the agent agrees to handle all incoming calls regarding property and will work with these prospective buyers and sellers to a positive outcome.

Fiduciary Relationship. A relationship between parties which is based on trust and confidence.

FSBO. See *For Sale By Owner.*

For Sale By Owner. A property which is offered for sale by the owner.

Homeowners Coverage. A form of insurance coverage available to homeowners for protection against loss to structure and/or contents.

Listing Agent. The agent responsible for the property on the market for sale or lease.

Listing Agreement. The contract between seller and agent establishing terms by which seller's property can be sold.

Listing Effort. Agent's efforts which, when successful, produce listings.

Listings. Properties offered for sale by real estate agents and companies.

MLS. See *Multiple Listing Service.*

Multiple Listing Service. A service which distributes on a regular basis information on all properties which are submitted by its members after they are listed by such members. The purpose is to make said properties available to the greatest number of people who are in a position to show them to prospective purchasers for the purpose of a sale.

Net Sheet. See *Estimated Closing Statement.*

Offer. The formal contract executed by a purchaser to offer to buy property of a seller.

Opportunity Time. See *Floor Time.*

People-to-People Public Relations. A system of consistently contacting individuals for the purpose of obtaining referrals.

Probate Attorney. Attorneys who specialize in settling estates.

Property Call. A call from a propsective purchaser or seller to a real estate office.

Property Time. See *Floor Time.*

P-T-P PR. See *People-to-People Public Relations.*

REALTOR®. A professional in real estate who subscribes to a strict Code of Ethics as a member of the local board and of the National Association of REALTOR®s.

Referral. Business which is referred to the agent by another individual.

Referral Agreement. An agreement between licensed real estate agents as to the terms by which they will work with one another regarding referrals.

Referral Fee. The amount of remuneration that licensed individuals agree to pay one another for referrals.

Referral Prospecting. Efforts made by an agent for the purpose of obtaining referrals.

Repeat Business. People who deal with the same agent as a result of positive past experiences with that agent.

Servicing. Servicing listings by notifying the sellers on a regular basis as to what has transpired relative to their property since the last contact.

Testimonial Letters. Letters from satisfied clients and customers expounding upon the virtues and talents of an agent and/or company.

Tickler File. A filing system whereby items are filed by days of the month, so that when each day begins the agent knows exactly what must be done based on the individual purpose of the file.

Tour. The scheduled time (usually each week) for every agent in the real estate office to preview the new listings which have been placed on the market since the last tour.

Index